Lean In

also by
April Poynter

Pressing Forward

Lean In
Chasing the Sunset

April Poynter

WordCrafts Press

To my dad, William H. Dotson
and to anyone who has chased the sunset
as they leaned in to the deep ache of loss and grief.

"The dark does not destroy the light; it defines it.
It's our fear of the dark that casts our joy into the shadows."
~Brene Brown

July 10, 2019

Suffering. It's part of life whether we like it or not.
Whether we want it or not.
The question is not 'how do I avoid suffering?'
The question is, 'how do I cope, move through and heal when suffering comes?'
Get off the sidelines.
Stop trying to avoid suffering.
It's bound to come.
It's guaranteed to strike.
But you don't have to stay pinned under the weight of it.
Stop playing it safe.
It's not safe.
Safety is an illusion and that's why you're so dissatisfied.
Freedom.
That freedom that you're searching for—
It's in the mystery.
That place you avoid most.
The scary place.
The dark corners that make you tremble with fear.
Freedom is there.
You're braver than you know.
Get off the sidelines and join this adventure called life.
Live life.
Lean into the discomfort.
Lean in to the thing that you so desperately fear.
The thing you've convinced yourself you could never endure.
The freedom is in the mystery.
Lean in.

I wrote those words 20 days before my family received life-altering news about my dad's health. It's amazing how sometimes our own hearts know exactly what we need to hear. I've often found myself sharing words with others, only to have them echo back to me when I need them most.

When my dad was diagnosed with colorectal cancer, I had already been on a journey of change for a couple of years—a journey that was far from complete. I was waking up to who I am. Old ideals were falling off, and this new concept of who I am was finding me.

But not as if I was discovering some new person. It's more like I was finding my way back home—if that makes sense.

A returning of sorts.

Walking with my dad through his cancer journey brought me face to face with what life really is all about—or what I think it's about—and it enriched the path of self-discovery I had already embarked upon.

I'm sure I'll continue to explore and learn more throughout my days. I'll have other experiences of mortality in the future. But there are certain truths and lessons that only find us when we are walking through the valley of the shadow of death.

These words you are about to read are how I grieved.

It's how I celebrated good news. It's how I processed difficult news.

Don't be surprised if you find a spicy F word ... or two ... or many. There are many.

You'll find contradictions and cussing all throughout.

You're following the thoughts of a real human with deep feelings who was grieving.

1

We grieve in many different forms.

I wrote. I held space for myself by writing.

By feeling every bit of everything there was to feel.

I documented the journey through my words. It was as if the words needed me. They came to me. They landed on me.

Some days I'd sit with words for hours. The passage wasn't long, but the space it created was necessary. Words would appear in my mind. Then tears would flow. One word could hold so much power. The meaning of that one word could untangle the despair that was all around me.

As I wrote and shared with the world through my social media outlets, I had people reach out to me and thank me for sharing my words.

They weren't just words for me.

They helped others. People who had been grieving for years but couldn't find the words to attach to their feelings and therefore could never release their grief.

The words had given them an opportunity to feel and release.

Grief comes in waves. We can't stop the waves. We can't control the waves.

But we can move with them.

Finding a flow of sorts.

The waves can be powerful, they're meant to be powerful. We're not trying to change the waves. We just need to change our stance among the waves.

Move.

Feel.

Flow.

I took the writings that I documented throughout my dad's cancer journey, and I compiled them here for you.

So that these words could be cast out into deeper waters—where you reside.

Throughout this book you'll be following that season through my eyes and from my perspective. Mostly watching my dad, but also living my life with the heaviness that comes along with cancer infiltrating someone you love.

Because.

Well.

Life goes on. It keeps going. The next day shows up and then the next one.

I wanted to capture all of it.

Including my dad's eulogy that you'll read first—I added a lot more in this book than I read at my dad's memorial service, but I've had some time to think and ponder since I originally wrote the eulogy. I felt there was more to share.

This book combines a journalism style writing with the eulogy that is later eclipsed by poetry. My true writing style is poetry. But I put my whole heart and soul into this eulogy and felt it was appropriate to share it here.

I'm grateful for the journey. I hope this book honors my dad's life and his death and whatever happens beyond. I'll leave that to your beliefs, thoughts, and imagination. But for me, there is something so beautiful and magical beyond what we see here in front of us. I know my dad has joined whatever that may be.

My ultimate hope for this book is that you would find the beauty between the light and dark as you navigate your journey.

Not necessarily a cancer journey, although this book is ripe for that. But for this journey of life.

Chasing the sunset is how I stayed present.

I chose not to get stuck focusing on what was. Or what might be. I chased the sunset.

Meaning, I knew the dark was coming. It was already moving in. I knew night would come soon.

But I made it my mission to find the beauty that only light and dark can make together.

There's beauty even in our darkest times.

Look for it. Believe for it. And lean into every ounce of it— as it's leaning into you.

Freedom is in the mystery.

Lean in.

When you hear about a cancer diagnosis, immediately your heart sinks.

Your brain is thrusted into thinking about death in a way you've never thought about it before.

It's in your face.

Front and center.

At first, when we found out that my dad had cancer, we wanted to look backwards.

If only he had gone to his preventative doctor appointments.

If only he had gone to the doctor when he started noticing something wasn't right within his body.

It didn't have to be this way.

He wouldn't have to fight this type of battle—

We wouldn't be feeling this way if only—

But looking backwards doesn't do much of anything except fill you with regret.

It leaves you longing for changes you can't make.

Looking back will paralyze you and render you useless.

My dad, my mom, my 2 brothers, Tony & Eric, and myself decided right away that we wouldn't start this journey by looking back. We were only looking forward.

Onward. Upward. But no looking back.

We would lean into all the discomfort. All the pain.

I decided early on that I wanted to watch the glorious unfolding.

I would keep my eyes open. I don't want to miss a thing.

I finalized this book two years after my dad passed away, and I can tell you—I have no regrets. I did not close my eyes. I did not—miss a thing.

My dad and I talked often about anxiety.

It's something he never understood. But back in 2011, my life changed drastically. I experienced my first panic attack. It was the scariest thing I had ever experienced. I didn't know what a panic attack was, so I assumed I was just dying. Until I went to the doctor, and they found nothing wrong with me.

Which made me more anxious, because what I had experienced wasn't *nothing*. It was very much *something*.

Death is what it was.

Call it what you want.

I called it death—except you're trapped alive while you're dying. For 365 days, I was stuck in a loop of anxiety and panic.

Come to find out, the panic attack scared me so badly, I was constantly fearing another one—so the anxiety loop kept me caught in a destructive cycle.

After a year of battling, I found my way out. I realized that when fear is staring us in the face, we want to resist. We tense up. We run the other direction. We do everything we can to avoid the discomfort.

But I learned through those 365 awful days, that you can't run from you.

I remember one day, my husband and I were house sitting for my in-laws while they were out of town. I drove home to get our pillows. I was in my apartment—alone. This dense cloud of fear came over me. I started running through the apartment to get our pillows and get the hell out of there.

I grabbed the pillows off of our bed and ran down the hallway to the living room. I stopped in the living room, threw the pillows to the floor, and fell to my knees and wept.

"What am I running from?" I asked myself in desperation.

"Where are you going?"

"This fear is in you. Not outside of you. You cannot escape it by running."

That day, I laid prostrate, with my face to the floor. I did the most terrifying thing. I chose to sit with the fear. I chose to let the feelings of anxiety freely move through my body—if it killed me; it killed me.

I leaned in.

It was the most terrifying experience. But I resolved that I would not run anymore.

My fingers tingled. My toes went numb. The sickness in my stomach was overwhelming. The panting of my breath was scary—but even so—I chose to let it happen. Let the waves of fear rush over me.

After the intensity of the feelings subsided, I laid on the floor for a little while longer.

I felt beat up and tired.

But no longer afraid.

I realized that day that the freedom we so desperately seek is on the other side of what we fear most.

It's not about running away.

It's about leaning in.

I learned that sometimes anxiety is a warning.

But oftentimes, anxiety is an invitation.

It calls out to us and invites us to go deeper.

It wants us to shake off things that we've attached to our identity— that causes us to live our lives as a lie.

It's asking us to stop betraying ourselves.

It's an invitation for abundance.

Clarity.

Restoration.

Fulfillment.

It's asking us to peel off the outer layers and step into the fullness of who we really are.

In 2017, I wrote a book about my experience.

It's called *Pressing Forward: Pushing Through Fear and Anxiety to Find My Truest Self.*

In a nutshell, the book says—lean in.

As I said, my dad never understood anxiety. He would say: "Why worry about shit you can't control? I just don't get it, Pearl (the nickname he gave me when I was a kid)."

No matter how much I tried to explain, he could not grasp what I was talking about.

My dad lived with a *lean-in* mentality. Maybe that's why he didn't experience or understand anxiety. He didn't resist when he faced challenges. He grew up in a generation where you plowed through.

He told me a story once about when he was a boy. He said there was a brick wall, and he told his mama, "I'll run right through that brick wall."

Her response—"You better not. I'll whip your ass."

A few things here to dissect:

First of all: This tells you about my dad. What kind of person is walking around wanting to run through brick walls?

What?

Why?

Gosh, I'm glad our kids have iPads and phones. Give me screen time—anytime.

Second: He was confident about being able to run through the wall. He was determined to run through it. He believed he could.

Third: His mother didn't tell him that the wall was made of brick. She didn't explain to him that his flesh and bone, regardless of how strong he was—would most likely be no match for that brick wall.

Instead—she told him, "You better not. I'll whip your ass."

My dad had no sense of "I can't." He didn't run through the wall—not because he believed he couldn't—but because he was scared of his mama and knew he'd get his tail beat if he ran through that wall.

That's how he was raised. That was his mindset. You just do what you gotta do.

Get into motion. Take action. Get to work.

My dad worked with his hands his whole life as a mechanic—but he lived in his head. Plowing through mental brick walls that make most of us stumble. He busted right through.

Throughout the 11 months of his cancer journey from diagnosis to his last breath, I referenced 'lean in' more times than I can count.

Because that's what those 11 months were.

Head first.

Leaning in.

Letting fear move through.

Not resisting.

No white-knuckling.

You can't grip what's fleeting no matter how hard you try.

And even if you brace for impact, the impact keeps coming.

Living your life constantly in a state of tension is no way to live at all.

It's not about running away.

It's about leaning in.

The pain is an invitation.

It calls out to us and invites us to go deeper.

Throughout this journey of 11 months, I saw my dad soften. Being a daddy's girl, I always saw a piece of him that was a little more tender than most people.

I'm the only girl.

And I'm the middle child.

Some call me "stubborn like my daddy."

I just say I'm "Strong-willed"—just like my daddy would say about himself.

I was in trouble a lot growing up.

Not because I was bad.

But because I was misunderstood.

Or—at least that's my story.

When I was 17 years old, I got in trouble (again). My dad was so fed up with me. But instead of taking his natural "you do what I say" approach (I am my father's daughter. Telling me what I'm going to do never works out well for anyone.) He sat me down and he said to me:

"If you were your child. What would you do with you?"

With tears in my eyes, I looked deeply into his eyes and I said, "I would listen to her. I'd stop talking *at* her and listen to what she thinks."

My dad took me to the back bedroom, away from everyone—and he gave me a hug. He held me tight for a few minutes. He told me he was hard on me because he cared about me.

I melted into his arms and wept.

Our relationship changed for the better that day.

My dad softened towards me.

I softened toward him.

We found a middle ground where both of our voices could be heard.

For the first time in my teen years, we were both leaning in toward each other.

We realized that opinions are opinions.

This doesn't mean someone is right or wrong.

We realized that I would be responsible for the choices I made. Good or bad. The outcomes would be mine. The consequences would be mine.

We realized that just because you don't agree with someone—doesn't mean you have to hate them.

And we realized that oftentimes neither of us understood the other—and that was okay too. You don't have to understand in order to love someone.

And sometimes if you love someone—you're actually a little more open to understanding.

Because if you stop saying what you so strongly disagree with—you might find yourself cracking open to new ideas and concepts and ways of life.

Like iced coffee for instance.

My dad never understood iced coffee.

He'd say,

"Why in the hell would you put ice in coffee? You drink it black. In the morning. Then you move on."

I'd say,

"Or... you can drink it with ice. You can drink it frosted. You can drink it with foam. Or cold foam.

"You can have it in the morning. Or mid-day. Or the afternoon. Yes—you can drink it black. Do that if it's your preference but until you've tasted an iced coffee with caramel syrup and almond milk on a hot summer's day—don't tell me you don't understand. Try it first. You don't have to understand it. But you have to at least try it.

"You can say, *I tried it once. It wasn't my thing. I didn't understand.* Not—*I don't understand.* You haven't *tried* to understand."

When my dad was going through chemo, I'd meet him for *Chemo Wednesday* every other week. We would sit together during infusion, just him and me. Afterwards, we'd meet my mom for lunch.

One day during chemo, my dad turned to me and said with a smirk on his face.

"I tried iced coffee."

"WHAT?!" I said in shock and disbelief!

"Did you like it?" I asked.

He smiled and nodded. "It was pretty damn good."

Seek first to understand, my friends.

Don't just dismiss what you don't understand.

You could be missing out on some of the most wonderful experiences in life because you're not willing to try before you dismiss what doesn't resonate with you right off.

Like hobbies.

Or food—so many wonderful foods.

Or even on a deeper scale—you could be missing out on people from different lifestyles, cultures, and backgrounds. Different upbringings and mindsets.

And most importantly you would miss out on iced coffee.

Don't miss out on iced coffee because you don't understand and you haven't tried to understand.

Food was a source of hope during my dad's journey. Chemo

destroys the pleasure of food. My dad didn't lose his appetite much during those 11 months, but his taste wasn't so lucky.

He constantly struggled to find things to eat that tasted good to him.

We always enjoyed an iced cold beer together before his cancer diagnosis. Even in the beginning of the cancer journey, we'd go to lunch and order Blue Moon, our favorite beer, on tap. Until one day neuropathy from chemo set in, and he couldn't drink cold beer anymore. I'd offer to call the restaurant and ask them to set a beer out to become room temperature before we arrived, but my dad didn't want to create an inconvenience, so he'd get water with no ice.

One day he was telling me about how meat was disgusting. No flavor. Just texture. And meat texture is not good with no flavor. Dad said to me, "I'm going to be really pissed if I have to be a vegan. Because that's not something I consider cool."

Then he goes, "Oh, bacon."

Me: "Bacon?"

He smiled. "Bacon is still bacon. It tastes just the same."

I want to encourage you—if for some reason you ever wind up getting chemo treatment and your taste is shot.

According to my dad, Bacon is still bacon. And how glorious is that?

During my dad's final few days on earth, we cherished and treasured our limited time with him. We were presented with a plethora of life lessons in a short amount of time.

Two days before my dad died, my older brother, Tony, came to the hospital to see him. When he came into the room there was a lot going on with the nurse checking in and getting medications for my dad. I watched Tony slowly fade into a corner of the room where he stood quietly and watched from a distance.

Tony is 20 months older than me. We have always been close. He's never known a time of being an only child without me, and I've never known a time without him.

On Tony's 18th birthday he shared with me that he was gay.

He was terrified to tell me. There was so much shame behind his words as he expressed his secret identity.

He cried as he told me.

I asked why he was so sad about it, and he shared that he thought I would not accept him anymore.

It was the year 2001. Things were not very progressive in our town, and minds were very much closed.

Prior to coming out to me, Tony had shared with my mom a year earlier. Throughout his senior year of high school he continued to share with more people and discovered that he was still loved and accepted by most. He did have his obstacles, bullies, and fair share of experiences with close-mindedness.

My mom told my dad.

My dad was one of those closed-minded people.

He didn't say much about it besides that he always knew Tony was *different*. From my perspective, not saying anything left a young boy in an unknown headspace about his identity when it came to his dad and whether or not his dad loved and accepted him *even if* he was gay.

Tony had never known exactly how my dad felt until my dad was a few days away from dying.

In that hospital room, just a few days away from his final breaths, my dad looked around and spotted Tony in the corner.

"Tony, get on over here," he said as he called Tony to him.

Tony walked over to the bed. My dad reached out, and Tony leaned in for a hug that was initiated by our dad.

They hugged tightly, and I heard my dad say to Tony, "I've always loved you, boy. Although I've never understood you."

Tony laughed and said, "Same!"

My dad was not a guy who threw 'I love you' around.

If he didn't mean it—he wouldn't say it.

But he also assumed people knew he loved them—and therefore he didn't say it.

We all needed to hear him say it. We got that opportunity, fortunately at the end of his life. Unfortunately—at the end of his life. We needed to know far before then. But we're grateful we got to know and hear it from him directly.

If you love people. Tell them.

Don't let gaps in your relationships create a distance between the exchange of 'I love yous.'

When you think of the people you love—if you think about telling them right now, "I love you" and that feels weird to you...

Fix it.

Fix whatever *that* is.

Because there's a wedge.

A similar situation happened between my husband, Tony, and my dad. Yes. My husband and my brother both are named Tony. So, hopefully this won't be too confusing.

Tony is a black man and at the time my dad was passing away we had been married for 15 years.

As my dad's time was drawing near, he requested that my husband come see him.

Tony had been covering at home and with our two kids so I could spend as much time with my dad as possible.

And to be honest, Tony and my dad weren't close.

They didn't *not* like each other.

They were cordial and respectful and spoke when they saw each other.

My dad asked if Tony would come to the hospital so he could talk to him face to face.

My dad was born in Texas and raised in Oklahoma. He was a good ol' country boy.

In my teen years we had a bit of conflict when it came to interracial dating.

I was never raised by my parents to see the world through a lens of skin color. But when I was in middle school and had a crush on a black boy, I got a lecture about how I could only be friends with him.

This made no sense to me, and I pushed back against it from that moment and through my teen years.

When I was 17, I was dating a black guy from my high school, and I talked to my dad about it.

For the first time, my dad sat and listened to me. We had a conversation that I'll never forget. I felt heard and understood. My dad asked to meet the guy, and I arranged it.

My dad met with the guy, and they clicked immediately.

Over the years I watched my dad's old belief system start to fall away. He allowed himself to change his mind and grow beyond his biases and limited thinking, and our relationship got better because of that.

When I met Tony my dad liked him. There were no objections. In fact, my dad would often reference that Tony reminded him of himself.

But they never got close.

They'd talk at family gatherings or sit together and watch whatever sports game was on TV, and every now and then they'd check out my dad's gun collection together and chat about their interest in firearms. But their relationship didn't extend beyond that.

When my dad was in the hospital, just hours away from death, Tony came to see him. I sat in the car with my son, Sway, so Tony and my daughter, Trinity, could have a few minutes alone saying their goodbyes. I purposely kept Sway at a distance because he was so young, and I didn't want him to see my dad in that condition.

My dad passed away a few hours later, my brothers and I spent time at my mom's house immediately after, and by the time I got home everyone was asleep.

It wasn't until later the next day that my husband got to share with me about his last conversation with my dad.

It takes a lot to get Tony a little shaken, but he was shaken. He had an opportunity to look into the face of a dying man and hear his final words to him.

And not just any dying man.

My dad.

Tony said my dad told him everything he needed to hear.

He didn't know how badly he needed to hear this, until he heard it.

My dad spent those moments with Tony telling him how proud he was of him. He thanked him for being a good husband and father. He let him know he was proud he was his son-in-law.

Ultimately, my dad let Tony know he accepted him for who he was.

Tony shared with me later that he figured my dad was good with him, but he just never really knew for sure.

So, after 15 years of being part of my family and just a few hours away from my dad's death, my dad cleared the air with my husband by telling him directly what he thought about him.

Tony said to me, "It feels good not to wonder, but instead know."

There is a lot to learn from this exchange.

Not everyone who is facing death gets to say what they need to say.

Say it now.

And remind them often.

I am so grateful that Tony and my dad got to have this interaction, and my biracial daughter got to witness it.

Whatever has stopped you from being vocal with those you love—break through that barrier.

Not only does it release you from all the things you haven't said; it frees them too.

My dad cut it close on this one. But he got to say it.

Let's not cut it this close in our own lives and risk the chance of never saying what needs to be said to those we love and admire.

A few hours after the conversation between my dad and my husband—my dad was gone.

Emptied of everything he needed to say to everyone he loved.

Him freed.

Them freed.

No need to wonder anymore.

Look around your life for the people in the corners.

Whether they were slowly pushed to a corner or slowly backed themselves into that corner—call them back.

Let them know there is no reason to hide or shy away.

Let them know you see them and want them near.

Let them know they are worthy to stand beside you.

Shame drives us to the corner. Guilt drives us to the corner. Fear that we're not fully accepted for who we are—pushes us into the corner.

All we ever really want to know is, "Do you see me? Do you hear me? Do you accept me? Do you love me? Do I matter?"

If someone you love gravitates near the corner in your presence, draw them out quickly and let them know they belong next to you regardless of your differences.

I mentioned earlier that my dad never understood anxiety. As his days were drawing near, my dad experienced his first panic attack. Think about it.

He was already having a hard time breathing due to his lungs—his colon cancer had metastasized and was in his lungs, which made him cough and lose his breath constantly. When my dad was in the hospital for the last time, one night—early morning, actually—around 4:00 AM, my dad had a coughing spell. These were quite common during the last few months. As he was having a coughing spell his oxygen dropped, then he had a bronchospasm, then he had a panic attack—unbeknownst to him.

Rightfully so.

The nurse called my mom—who was at home because my dad told her to stay there and get some rest—and said that my dad was scared and wanted her to come to the hospital. In a matter of 15 minutes after that phone call, my mom was by his side.

When I got to the hospital later that day, it was just me and my dad in the room. He told me about his experience that morning. Then he turned to me and said, "That was the scariest thing I've ever gone through." As he explained the details, I realized he had experienced a panic attack.

He said, "I've always been able to tell my brain—'Stop.' 'Calm down.' 'You're okay.'—but this time, my brain was not listening."

My dad had spent a few days in the hospital just a week prior to his *final* stay. We thought that was the end for him, but he bounced back and went home for a couple of days before returning for his final stay. During that previous time in the hospital while he was bedridden, nowhere to go—I brought my book, *Pressing*

Forward, to him and *made* him read it. It wasn't to help him. He wasn't experiencing anxiety at that time. I made him read it for my own selfish reasons.

I figured he had never read my book as most close friends and relatives don't read their author friend's books.

We literally have to find you bedridden to make you read our stuff. Do better, y'all.

Kidding.

But am I?

My dad had nowhere to go, and he read my book in a day.

When I came to visit him the next day, he pulled the book from a drawer on his side table, and he handed it back to me.

"Here. I read it," he said.

I got all sappy, as if he voluntarily read it on his own, and I didn't force it on him.

"Awwww, you read my book."

He didn't have to read it. But he did.

He responded, "Yup. I still don't get it. But I read it."

And now here we were, a week later. He fully understood.

I mean, I guess I need to reference the fact that most people experience anxiety in cases such as:

I don't think my boss likes me. Anxiety.

Am I going to get fired? Anxiety.

I'm going to be late. Anxiety.

I'm worried about the thing that will probably never happen. Anxiety.

No reason at all. Anxiety.

But my dad—literally staring death in the face. Anxiety.

Show off.

Don't worry. As he shared his horrifying experience with me, I didn't pity him. Instead I looked him in the face, folded my arms and went, "Well, well, well.... Look who met anxiety?" I chuckled at him. "I'd say you understand now, huh?"

"Yup." He grinned and nodded.

"Good thing you read my book," I said back to him, smiling.

I got to spend the next few minutes coaching him through anxiety and panic attacks. I hoped to help relieve the fear by explaining to him how it works. Once anxiety strikes, it can't stay heightened and it has to move. No matter how scary it may seem when it first hits, it loses its grip as it moves.

Anxiety is energy. It simply needs to move.

Later that day, my dad was prescribed anti-anxiety medication. The night was daunting to him because he was afraid he'd go through that terror again. He was very open about his fears at this point.

Here's what I learned from that experience.

I spent a year suffering through anxiety and panic attacks in 2011. Nine years later, I was at my dad's bedside coaching him through anxiety and panic attacks.

You can't give what you don't have.

I battled anxiety. It almost took me out, but I overcame it. And because of that horrible experience of my own, I was able to comfort and coach my dad.

Nine years later.

The hardships that we experience are never void.

Nothing is lost.

We may not always understand why we're going through what we're going through. And I'm not saying we're going through it specifically to help other people later.

No. Sometimes we go through hard things because that's just life. I don't believe "all things happen for a reason." I just believe it's part of being human, and we're having a human experience.

Good experiences. Bad experiences. Label them if you want or just call them what they are—*experiences*.

Living.

Being human.

Each challenge and opportunity is offering us growth and expansion. Depending on your mindset, you can walk away with treasures and new tools in your toolbox. Overcoming our past hardships can be the ticket of hope that someone else needs while they're in the thick of their hardship.

Nothing is lost.

No experience is ever void.

A couple of hours before my dad passed away, my brothers, Tracy (my dad's boss and friend), and I were in the room talking with my dad.

Although he did have a morphine drip, my dad was not *drugged*. He actually seemed very normal considering the circumstances. At one point during our conversation I said something about how my dad should take an edible—medicinal, of course—but then I joked and said, "Never mind, you're already on the good stuff—morphine."

Dad's voice broke through and said, "Hell, I'm already seeing hummingbirds."

All the eyes in the room shifted toward him.

"You're seeing hummingbirds?" I asked.

"Yeah. If you see me doing this"—pulling his head back—"it's because they keep flying by my head."

Then he carried on as if what he had just shared with us was completely normal.

But the rest of us were stunned.

Later, I looked up the symbolism of seeing hummingbirds, and I found some really neat articles. I'm sure most wouldn't believe the details, but for me, there's just something so mysterious and magical about the symbolism. Here are some key points from the article I found on *thesecretofthetarot.com/hummingbird-spirit-animal/*

"When the hummingbird comes into your life, be ready to receive wisdom and insight. This spirit animal has a special role that it plays in the animal kingdom.

For example, it enables you to connect with your inner being. It delivers spiritual messages to guide you on how to go about this.

The hummingbirds move in a unique pattern. Their pattern brings to mind the concepts of infinity, continuity, and eternity.

A close look at the hummingbird reveals that these birds do not tire easily. They will be busy looking for the sweetest nectar available in their environment.

The hummingbird in your life is a sign of love and happiness. It appears as a miracle of life.

Its presence wants you to know that the sweetest nectar is within your reach.

More importantly, you can access this nectar from deep within you. Therein lies your most powerful resources.

This bird is known to fly far and wide. When it flies into your life, you get the ability to withstand challenging journeys with much joy.

The hummingbird teaches you to be independent. It empowers you to cherish being in the present moment.

People with this image learn quickly to enjoy life. They are not encumbered by the worries of this world. They know the value of life.

The hummingbird encourages you to let light into your life.

If the hummingbird is your companion, you'll be able to fly from one place to the next with good cheer.

Just like the hummingbird, you have the innate desire to be free. You are resilient and fierce. You will travel without boundaries.

The hummingbird opens your eyes to the value of your loved ones. You are able to appreciate them more.

You have the ability to adapt to whatever changes that come your way.

When you make contact with the hummingbird, know that the journey ahead of you will be lighter. You will be equipped with the tools you need on this journey.

The hummingbird symbol is about your perseverance and endurance.

It empowers you to experience more love, more joy, and more happiness as you journey along. This is the magic of life.

With this magic, your life becomes more fulfilling.

With time, you are able to achieve what other people can only dream of.

The hummingbird spirit animal perches in your life to add value. It is showing that you are a messenger of jubilation and hope. Thus, you act as an inspiration to those who are watching you.

Sometimes we get a beating from life, and we lose our original focus.

This is where the hummingbird comes in. It helps you to refocus. In this way, you become more productive in your endeavors.

The hummingbird opens your gateway to true happiness and joy.

The hummingbird appears in your life just at the right moment, when you need it most. It may come to you in the form of a sighting, as a vision, or in a dream.

Hummingbird symbolism is reminding you that that joy is just around the corner. Stop waiting and go. Alternatively, the hummingbird meaning is letting you know that you can go anywhere you desire. The only obstacle in your way is yourself."

I read this to my mom and my brothers shortly after my dad passed. We were all stunned and yet filled with so much hope.

I'll never look at hummingbirds the same.

None of us will.

So, if you see one on your journey—remember its meaning and find hope in any challenge you may be facing—knowing you are fully equipped and capable—and most likely, standing in your own way.

I want to share with you a moment that will be stained in my heart forever.

When my dad started his transition, it lasted an hour and 15 minutes.

Then he was gone.

Earlier in the day, we were talking to the palliative care PA. With my dad listening, the PA told us that because my dad wasn't expelling carbon dioxide properly, eventually he would start to get drowsy, then extremely drowsy and start to fall asleep. As he drifted off to sleep without waking back up, the medical team would administer sedation medication. Once he was in complete slumber, she suggested that we pull the oxygen from his nose and let his body naturally die.

For my dad, it would be peaceful.

For us, it would be hard to watch.

Damn, was it hard to watch.

Because my dad—William Dotson—was literally stubborn, I'm sorry, *Strong-Willed*, all the way up to his his last breath.

He did get drowsy.

But his transition was fast. He never asked for the sedation medication. Maybe because he didn't know the transition was happening, but most likely because he was going to do things on his terms.

That's just who he was.

Even up to death.

He was going to have a say so.

I wouldn't expect any less from him.

Just to give you a glimpse into the room during that final hour and 15 minutes, specifically the last 20 minutes.

It was not peaceful—at first.

In fact, it was awful.

Chaotic.

Scary.

Unsettling.

Disturbing.

Commotion.

His diaphragm working overtime to make him breathe.

Watching his body fight—not to die—but to live. Because we are wired to live.

And watching his nurse try her hardest to settle his reactions with numerous vials that she quickly shot into his IV.

She was chasing him down.

The medicine was following him.

But he was running the show.

Moments before he passed, he weakly reached his hand up. We weren't sure what he was about to do, but what he did next moved us all to tears, including the nurses that were now watching from the back of the room.

He reached one hand up to his right ear, and he removed the oxygen tube from around it.

Then he slowly reached up to the left ear and tugged at the tube. He was too weak and disoriented, but I could see he was trying to remove it, so I said, "You want it off, Dad?"

With no expression on his face, I could barely see him nod, yes.

"Here. I got it," I said.

And I pulled it off of his left ear.

He then reached up, and *he* removed the oxygen tube from his nose.

Stubbornness or strong will or whatever you want to call it—my dad made his own decision.

He knew the oxygen was prolonging the dying experience.

He didn't need us to pull the oxygen from his nose. He'd do it himself.

I believe he was letting us know, *I'm done.*

It was the most beautiful moment in the midst of our hearts breaking.

I wish I could say, 'and then he slowly drifted off to his final slumber, peacefully.'

But not quite yet.

Shortly after he removed the oxygen, he tried to sit up. Some may say he wasn't aware at this point, but I saw his eyes.

He had one more moment of panic.

Sheer terror.

He could not breathe, and he wanted to sit up. Through what was left of his shallow breath he mumbled, "I need to sit up."

With one hand behind his head and one hand on his chest, I gently pushed him back against the bed and said, "Daddy. It's okay. We're all here with you. Let go."

And he did.

He let go.

He stepped over the threshold.

He broke through the veil.

It was the ultimate *Lean in.*

And peace flooded the room.

Peace that passes all understanding.

Peace that makes no sense.

Peace that you can't explain with words—you can only feel it with your heart.

One of those—*you had to be there to get it*—moments.

But my mom, my brothers, and I all felt it on a cellular level. We felt it in our being.

We knew he was at peace. We were at peace.

A little traumatized—but we'll work through that.

Here's what I learned:

There is no pretty way to die.

Death is not pretty.

But honestly, neither is birth.

Yet, we talk about the birth of a baby as this glorious, beautiful event.

No way. Birth is awful.

Chaotic.

Scary.

Unsettling.

Disturbing.
Commotion.
It's gross.
Disgusting things are happening.
Fluids are flying.
Monitors are beeping.
The body is fighting to bring in life.
There's nothing pretty about it.
But once the baby has arrived and takes that first breath—
Peace.
It floods the room.
Peace that passes all understanding.
Peace that makes no sense.
Peace that you can't explain with words—you can only feel it
with your heart.
One of those—*you had to be there to get it*—moments.
And what was once awful, horrifying, gross, disturbing, chaotic,
scary as hell—takes on the image of beauty.
What was traumatizing fades. Like a distant memory. As if that
part never happened.
And we're left with the illumination of glory.
Death is no different than birth.
Whether life is coming or going—there is beauty to be found.
There's beauty in the full cycle of life.

I miss my dad. Those 11 months, although trying, were filled with
so many wonderful moments.

Those 11 months softened him. Cracked him open so we could
know him more. I learned more about him in those few months
than I knew my whole life. He just wasn't one to talk about himself.

The day before he died, my brother, Tony, was sitting with him
and found out my dad had been reading a book series for 20 years,
The Dresden Files by Jim Butcher. There was a summer release of
the newest book coming out on July 14, 2020. My dad shared with

Tony that he was pissed he wouldn't get to read it. He had waited four to five years for that new book.

Tony took it to Twitter in hopes that his tweet and his community retweeting and tagging the author would get Jim's attention and get my dad an advanced copy of the book, *Peace Talks*.

Within a few hours, Tony received a message from Jim's associate.

```
Hey Tony, tell your dad he's in luck.
Jim wants to hook him up with both
PEACE TALKS and BATTLE GROUND, the
two Dresden Files novels coming out
this summer. I'll make it happen!
```

We were all in tears when this message came through. Then Tony told my dad.

My dad was elated.

"I'll be damned," he said.

Then a few minutes later, "I'll be damned."

He could not believe it.

Tony set it up so that my dad could listen to the book on audio and let it play while he rested in the hospital bed.

As my dad was drifting into his final slumber, he reached up to try to turn the speaker down a little. I asked what he needed help with. He said, "Turn it down a little." I paused the audio. In the silence, I looked at him sleeping and started to quietly cry.

His eyes opened quickly, and he snapped at me. "April. Turn it back on. I just want you to turn it down a little."

"Okay, okay, Dad!" I hurried to turn it back on while my brothers and I busted into laughter.

He was so adamant about listening to those books before his time ran out.

After he had passed, the room was silent—only the book audio playing softly. My mom, brothers, and I huddled around one another and cried together. No words, just the audio still playing in the background.

Jim's creativity is an extension of him—and it was everything we needed with us during this most difficult time.

We are grateful for the energy Jim poured into those books.

It not only inspired my dad and my family but it should inspire the creativity in all of us.

A reminder that our work matters far beyond what we could ever imagine.

A reminder that we are touching others in ways we may never know.

A reminder that our words and our creativity are a gift that we release. And it takes on an energy of its own once we part from it.

I remember when I was about to submit my book, *Pressing Forward*, to the publisher for the final time.

This was it.

No more edits.

No more changes.

No more critiquing.

I got stuck.

I couldn't submit it—

What if I missed one misspelled word? (Which I did, by the way.)

What if there's a part that doesn't make sense? Or I could tailor it a little better for the reader?

What if I forgot something?

What if I used the wrong word and diluted a sentence that was supposed to create more impact?

My publisher said the most profound thing to me.

He said, "April. Art was never meant to be perfected. It was only ever meant to be abandoned."

May my dad's journey be a reminder to us all that we should live while we're living.

Or—

Depending on how you look at it—we should all live while we're dying.

Because we're all dying, we just don't have a diagnosis and a prognosis and medical professionals directing our path, reminding us that we're dying.

And maybe these moments right here—honoring my dad's life, fully aware of his death, rightfully bring us face to face with where we're all headed at some point or another.

It's a moment for a heart check.

Are you happy where you are?

Are you at odds with someone and you miss them? But you're too stubborn or strong-willed to reach out and work it out?

Work it out.

Trust me when I tell you—work it out.

Do you overthink, over catastrophize, and keep yourself limited and stuck?

Let this be a reminder to stop.

May we treat our hindrances like art. Not to be perfected, but to be abandoned.

Over and over and over again.

And when we come upon those obstacles that lock us up in terror and make us want to run away

—and we will face those obstacles.

We surely will.

May we feel that fear—

Not labeling it as good or bad.

Not letting it stop us.

And remember that the freedom we so desperately seek is on the other side of what we fear most.

It's not about running away.

It's about leaning in.

As I said before—sometimes anxiety is a warning.

But oftentimes, anxiety is an invitation.

It calls out to us and invites us to go deeper.

It wants us to shake off things that we've attached to our identity that causes us to live our lives as a lie.

It's asking us to stop betraying ourselves.

It's an invitation for abundance.

Clarity.

Restoration.

Fulfillment.

It's asking us to peel off the outer layers and step into the fullness of who we really are.

Just as my dad did at the end of his life.

He pressed through fear and anxiety, and he found his truest self.

May these 10 learned lessons always be in the forefront of our minds:

1. Don't spend your time looking backward.
2. Run through the brick walls.
3. Seek first to understand. Don't miss out on iced coffee.
4. Be encouraged that bacon is still bacon—even if your taste buds burn off.
5. Call those you love out of the corners.
6. No experience is void.
7. Watch for the hummingbirds and the messages they bring.
8. Art was never meant to be perfected—only abandoned.
9. Anxiety is an invitation. Keep Pressing Forward.
10. Freedom is on the other side of what you fear most.

Lean in.

This part of the book is a mix of poetry and journal writings. These were written from July 2019—July 2021.

You'll follow my dad's journey, our feelings, our grief, our wins and losses, and what might seem like some random topics throughout this section of the book.

Feel free to follow it in order or bounce around to see what might be speaking directly to you.

Many of these words go far beyond my particular situation and I think—

I think they'll meet you where you're at on your path.

These words are my gift to you.

Take what you need.

I've learned that the tighter I grip something—the further it gets from me.

Fleeting.

Transient.

Pain is inevitable. Sorrow walks hand in hand with joy.

All the remnants of the unknown continue to knock.

And we call this life.

Capricious.

Shifting.

A constant scavenger hunt filled with beauty. Yet beauty often shines from among the rubbish.

Don't look away just 'cause it hurts.

Trust me. To hurt is better than to feel nothing at all.

Breathe in.

Breathe out.

Life. Another moment of life. Another breath not to be taken for granted.

This is living.

For today. For this moment.

Soak it up.

Keep living. Even when it hurts.

Without darkness—sunset would not be so beautiful.

Without darkness—sunrise would be dull.

Vast colors echo through the sky just before they're kissed and immersed by darkness.

I'm hopeful.

I'll embrace this darkness. Running straight into it with no resistance. Just as night and day collide for the beauty they can only create together.

No resistance.

The freedom is in the mystery.

I have cancer.

A text I got from my dad after the results from his biopsy came in.

We assumed this, but we hadn't gotten the results from the biopsy yet, and therefore, we hoped the results would prove us and the doctors wrong. But it didn't.

I never knew how to relate to a person with anxiety until I had my own season of anxiety and depression. Same with suicide. I could never understand until I walked through my own journey.

I've made it this far with healthy parents, siblings, husband, children.

Until now.

The other night, after a busy day with my parents—including

doctors, hospitals, pre-op admission, scheduling, insurance, disability claims and Nashville traffic—I laid down in bed around 11 PM. I closed my eyes after a day of feeling nothing, and tears poured out.

I just felt gratitude.

Overwhelming gratitude.

For 12 hours with my parents. We laughed and joked and picked on my dad. Even the medical staff joined us in teasing him.

We were together.

I was able to serve them in a way I have never been able to serve them.

I looked back throughout the day in my memories and saw the freedom that was present all day.

I cried tears of gratitude for all the moments leading up to this moment. I cried tears of gratitude for the journey we are leaning into. Because why not? We can't stop it. We can't go back. We can't wish for a different outcome.

All we have is here and now.

Not tomorrow. Or the what-ifs. Or the how-comes.

Not whether my dad lives or dies. Not whether he has to have chemo or not. Not whether this cancer has metastasized or not. We don't have any of that.

Just this moment.

And this one.

And this one.

That's it.

But that's life.

There is a storyline written for you within the cloud of your culture. When we hear, *cancer*, the programming tells you to jump into the stream of misery and death as if it's all over.

But I step back and watch that stream with its violent current rushing by. I'm not stepping into that current. I'm staying right here. Evaluating how I'm feeling. What I'm thinking. And letting it flow appropriately through me. On my terms.

And today—I'm grateful. Not because of cancer but I'm grateful for the depth of the conversations I've been able to have with people who have walked this journey before—regardless of the outcome of their experience.

A lady said to me yesterday, "I've been there." And I felt less alone. I felt like she understood something on a deeper level. She didn't try to fix it or move me through it. She didn't offer advice or say much of anything. Just—"I've been there."

And that was comforting.

I'm grateful for the journey we are on. Light and dark contrasting. Just like it always does. Creating beauty—just like it always does.

Don't get so consumed by the darkness that's approaching that you miss the beauty of the sunset behind you.

Stay in the moment.

So what if fear is present? Why wouldn't it be? Who said it shouldn't be?

Feel it.

Feel that too.

The sensations of emotion are reminding you that you're alive. That you're breathing. That your nervous system is in tune with you.

Don't rush. Don't try to change it. Let it be. Relinquish the need to control.

Where surrender resides, freedom will be found in that very place.

I'm suiting up and going in.

Dad, you may have cancer. But cancer don't have you.

Our pain creates a trench.

A hidden place that's easy to overlook when life is normal and on track.

But when you're in the valley, down in the trench, you tend to find a population of people there.

Trench dwellers.

Where were they before the news of my dad's diagnosis?

It's like they saw one of their own from a distance and rushed to take me in and suit me up for battle. Giving me the weapons and supplies they knew I'd need for the journey.

It's hard to find words that make sense.

I guess what I'm trying to say is:

If you're a trench dweller, a soldier, a warrior who has walked this journey or is walking this journey—I'm so sorry you've had to go through this. I know there are a plethora of feelings, emotions, and all kinds of other things that strike alongside a cancer diagnosis.

But I am so so so grateful for you. Because of what you've been through—you're equipped with a gift—a set of superpowers, really. And I can only hope that I can do for others what you have done for me.

You have no idea.

Thank you from the depths of everything I am.

~Your fellow trench dweller.

Night time brings moments of heavy grief for me. It comes in waves and it passes.

And I feel every bit of it.

Early detection and prevention would most likely not have us right here, right now.

But we are where we are.

We can't go back. We can't fix what's already been done. We pick up the pieces and go from here.

If you've been putting off an appointment, please go. Make it a priority.

Even if you're trying to avoid hearing bad news... please go.

My dad regrets not going to a doctor sooner.

And that breaks all of our hearts.

No one wants to live with regret.

I can only imagine the heaviness and defeat my dad is feeling right now.

He not only feels it.

Our whole family is aching because of it.

Get yourself checked out and don't delay any longer.

Work can wait. You can find time.

Do it.

I'm glad my dad wasn't *too late*—but he sure came close.

The tumor was five inches long and had grown through his colon and was sitting on a major artery. The surgeon took a major risk by removing it. But he was successful.

Unfortunately, even with the removal—

the cancer had already spread.

And when this deep grief hits me all I can think about is how I wish my dad would have gone to the doctor sooner.

I cry.

Then gently bring myself back to the present moment.

All we have is here and now.

My dad is here.

Right now.

And for that... I am grateful.

W hen you cry, don't hide or apologize.

Why would we stop ourselves from crying?

Why would we apologize?

You're crying because you're feeling. And feeling is part of being human. It's part of being alive. And being alive is a gift.

There are already too many of you walking around with suppressed feelings.

This is causing you to have resentments that are making you toxic.

It's causing you to have physical sickness in your body.

It's causing you to live a life in a constant state of fight or flight. You run and hide, or you're quickly offended and wound others through the lens of your own wounds.

Stop stopping yourself from crying. And stop apologizing for feeling.

I'm overwhelmed with emotion right now. And it's painful.

I'm not crying because I'm scared. Or because I need encouragement. Or because I feel hopeless.

I'm crying because my dad has been given a fucked up diagnosis and he's enduring some heavy shit right now. I'm weeping because this sucks. It really sucks for a human—a living, breathing, soul-filled human—who has to walk through this season.

I'm weeping because of the lack of information we have. And even if we had it—would it matter?

I'm weeping for the "I love yous" we're exchanging—heavier than we ever did before. And the weight those words carry when someone you love is battling for their life.

It's like a trail of footprints in fresh snow—and I'm begging the snow to stop falling so it won't cover the footprints as if they never existed. But the snow keeps falling.

I have to feel that.

I choose to watch it erase what was once there—and refuse to look away.

And I have to let myself feel that.

I'm weeping because I'm allowing myself to feel. I'm feeling because I'm human. Because I'm alive and feeling is not something we should ever run from—but something we are to embrace and move with.

Like a dance.

Like a bride dancing with her daddy at her wedding reception.

Feeling.

Moving through.

Dancing.

Weeping.

Tonight I'm reminded of two powerful words in the Bible. "Jesus wept." This gem is tucked in the story of Lazarus' death. Jesus shows up on the scene, and people are crying. They're not apologizing for their tears. They're hurting, and they're feeling all their emotions. And they're crying.

The scripture says that Jesus saw Lazarus' sister weeping, and friends who had come along with her were also weeping. Jesus was deeply moved in spirit and troubled.

Then that powerful, two-word scripture:

Jesus wept.

It's okay to cry. It's okay to feel what you need to feel. Why do you think we're a bunch of people now talking so openly about mental health issues and getting back to our *true, authentic selves?*

Because we have bottled up trauma and have suppressed our emotions.

We've lost sight of the footprints. We've become too stiff and embarrassed to dance. We don't want to move through—we want to find a shortcut around.

But what if we sat with our darkness? What if we cried, unapologetically?

I also believe those 2 words are powerful with any name. Put your name next to *wept* and end it with a period.

April wept.

Put your name there and feel the feelings:

_____ wept.

Do you feel that?

Now breathe.

Don't apologize.

Don't brace for impact.

Just breathe and sit with it.

Those feelings are not necessarily good or bad—they just are.

And they're okay.

The other day at work, during our all-staff Monday Huddle, I was giving my weekly update to the team. It was right after missing a few days due to my dad's surgery. I started talking to our team and immediately started crying. It came out of nowhere... and it was in a professional setting.

But I just cried.

I wept.

I was hurting.

And that team around me cried too.

They hurt for me.

Alongside me.

And there was something healing about that.

Us weeping together.

There are a lot of reasons to apologize, friends. But crying isn't one of them.

A white feather that mysteriously appears out of nowhere holds a message for me.

This started happening a few years ago. I haven't shared my white feather story with many people—but the gist of the message is;

It's okay.

I see you.

You're human.

You don't have to strive, or beg, or fight…

You just simply need to be you.

Right where you are.

In your humanity.

Gifts will be given without your agenda or interference.

The universe has you.

Recently I experienced a deep revelation. It shook me to the core and gave me insight and clarity that I had been chasing after for quite a while.

That evening, I was taking a walk, treasuring the revelation in my heart, when I looked down and saw a white feather.

It always shows up when I least expect it—right on time.

You are enough.

You can plan and map out a future that you desire—but don't lose yourself in it.

What you truly desire is not out there. It's in you. It always has been.

What you carry in your heart will draw in what you want *out there*.

You are who you're looking for. You're calling yourself back—and that's scary because it requires laying down things that helped you get to where you are now, but you can't take those things with you into your future.

Ideology.

Concepts.

Perceptions.

Assumptions.

Habits.

Traditions.

Even people.

It requires you to speak up. Take risks. You risk being judged. You risk people not liking you anymore. You risk people misunderstanding your heart and motives—

And you have to find a way to be okay with that.

It hurts.

Bad.

I know. I've been there and am still there. It's painful to be judged or misunderstood. It's even more painful to know the truth and intentionally decide not to share it.

To let people have the freedom to think what they want and let it be so.

That's hard. Painful. Risky. And it takes great courage. You have to be comfortable with your own resolve.

Life can be hard and incredibly complicated. But I promise you, the more you awaken your true essence, the richer your life becomes.

The journey is the destination.

The destination is you.

You're finding your way back to you.

If you pity my dad or offer your condolences the first thing he'll say is—"That's just life." And not in some apathetic, who gives a fuck type of way. But in a, 'this is where we're at for this part of my life with my decisions and it's how the cookie crumbles.'

He just goes with it.

He shows up for his appointments with the best attitude. I've heard him tell every doctor he's talked to, "I'm here for whatever we gotta do." No extra emotion. No what ifs… no sharing of regrets… just here and now. Rollin' with it.

Today, I walked into the room where he was getting his chemo administered and as soon as I saw him I felt hopeful.

He had color.

His eyes were normal.

He smiled and, upon seeing me, immediately became the little smart ass that he is.

Lively.

Still ill. But, damn. To see life in his eyes. What a gift.

I was driving to his appointment this morning and thinking about life. Thinking about this season. Thinking about how people tell me I'm so strong and positive. And how we reference this is *hard* or *tough*. In the words of my dad, "That's just life."

Strong is going to work on days when depression is kicking your ass. Strong is smiling when you want to break down and cry but need to hold it together. Strong is speaking in front of a large crowd when your knees are shaking.

Strong is saying I'm sorry to someone and not expecting acceptance or an apology back.

Strong is asking for help.

Strong is eating—not because you're hungry but because you know your body needs nutrition.

Strong is saying no. Without an explanation.

Strong is demanding respect. Setting boundaries—even when it tears your heart out because you know it can cost you relationships.

Strong is changing your mind. Being comfortable with your resolve. Not apologizing for who you are and what you need.

Strong is when you take a stand for the underdog. Being a voice for the voiceless.

It's choosing not to honk at the asshole who just cut you off in traffic and considering that maybe that *asshole* may have not seen you. Or maybe that *asshole* is numb from some news they just found out...

And perhaps that *asshole* isn't an asshole at all. But just another human. In their own world. Maybe their actions have absolutely nothing to do with *you*.

Strong is spending time alone and letting whatever comes to the surface—come to the surface.

Strong is part of life. But so is weak. And what exactly is weak?

Strong and weak are dark and light. Contrasting. Working together to create depth and beauty.

Just like the sunset.

Just like the sunrise.

Like beautiful art.

You can't have one without the other.

Strong is wanting it all.

The depth. The contrast. The beauty of dark and light.

There's a scripture in the Bible that says power is made perfect in weakness. For when I am weak, then I am strong.

The Apostle Paul was onto something there.

Whatever you're going through today—do it how you know how. Don't worry about strong or weak or any other word for it.

Go with your heart. Go with your gut. Go with the natural reaction—the voice inside of you that sounds like a faint and muzzled scream. Let that come out.

That voice is directing you.

And I'm pretty sure it's trying to reassure you by saying, "Keep living, my friend. Keep feeling. Keep going. That's just life. Go live the hell out of it."

Today is a good day.

Here's the thing about being in battle:

As much as you want to win. You strive to win. You believe you'll win.

The truth is—you just don't know what the end result will be.

You know you'll show up. Give it your all. Fight with everything you have.

But what if ultimately that's just not enough?

What if your best is not enough?

What happens when the motivation runs dry, and the positive affirmations leave you empty-handed?

And who says fighting is always fists and weapons? Why can't fighting be stillness and presence?

Or maybe it is.

Maybe victory is in the eye of the beholder.

Maybe it changes by the day.

By the moment.

By the second.

I wonder what would happen if we dropped our preconceived notions and contextual viewpoints of war.

And battle.

And victory.

And defeat.

Letting the true definitions shine through based off of our own personal journeys without comparison or judgment.

Forget what you know. Or what you've been taught or programmed to believe.

What does victory mean to you?

And you?

And you?

For me, sometimes winning is laying my weapons down.

Sometimes it's glaring adversity in the face, sword raised, and charging full force.

Sometimes it's sweat, blood, mud, tears.

Sometimes it's tidy and contained—but unraveling slowly and quietly.

An undoing of sorts.

Yet, still a victory.

Today, during my dad's appointment with the pulmonologist, we had a victory. We were told the cancer had not overtaken his lungs. In fact, his lungs were fine. The doctor suspects some damage occurred from the intubation during my dad's colorectal surgery that took place back when he first found out he had cancer.

He needs to see an ENT Specialist now to assess the nerve damage and work towards a solution to the chronic bronchial spasms he's been having nonstop for over a month.

This is a victory.

The war today consisted of asking the doctor lots of questions, telling a clear and concise story so the doctor could understand the series of events leading up to the chronic cough.

It ended with his lungs "sounding and looking fine" per the pulmonologist.

After the appointment we walked through the parking lot and celebrated a small win. We laughed, hugged, and made jokes.

Without concern for who may be watching, I raised my arms and let out a, "Woo hoo!" victory scream.

My dad still has cancer. He still has a long road ahead. And ultimately, the thing we dare not say—but I will—this cancer could potentially take his life.

That part of the story is still unwritten.

I don't need to know the end result.

Not today.

But here's what I do know:

For me, sometimes winning is laying my weapons down. Sometimes it's glaring adversity in the face, sword raised, and charging full force. Sometimes it's sweat, blood, mud, tears. Sometimes it's tidy and contained—but unraveling slowly and quietly.

An undoing of sorts.

Sometimes it's drawing near to the enemy—in peace.

Regardless of the risk.

Sometimes there are no weapons drawn at all. Just me and darkness, face to face. I'm trembling but not backing down.

Still a victory. In its own time.

We can't say what the *end* victory looks like, because we're not there yet.

Here's what I think I know:

Victory has never been about life or death.

Winning or losing.

It's the storyline of the in-between.

Taking that first terrifying trip to the doctor. The visit he had put off for months because he didn't want to hear what he already knew. He didn't want it confirmed.

Processing the idea that he had a tumor—that was most likely cancerous.

Having numerous tests done, at different places, with different doctors.

Being plucked from work abruptly.

Hearing the confirmation that he did have cancer.

Colorectal surgery where the tumor was supposed to be removed but instead, during the procedure the surgeon saw the cancer had already spread, and he suggested—during surgery while my dad was under—that my dad get a colostomy, which we told him about two hours post surgery. He had absolutely no idea prior to us telling him.

Being told the cancer was stage 4.

Discovering he had declined Short Term Disability and Long Term Disability during his recent benefits open enrollment.

Developing a cough that wouldn't go away. Over the weeks it ultimately progressed to chronic bronchial spasms. If you've ever had bronchitis, you know how this literally stops your life and limits all physical activity.

Outpatient surgery for insertion of his chemo port.

First round of a five-hour chemo infusion.

Being told the cancer had spread to his lungs.

Being told the cancer was not overtaking his lungs, but his vocal cords/bronchial tube may have nerve damage.

Not to mention him learning to live with a colostomy bag and all it entails.

Trying to take a quarter of a mile walk when he can't breathe properly—with an inhaler in his hand.

Making me and himself breakfast on a Saturday morning with a "burnt brain" from chemo.

Surviving on two to four hours of sleep per night—and all the other challenges that fill those 24 hours each day.

These things make up the storyline of the *in-between.*

Along with the laughter. The jokes. Hearing stories about him that I've never heard before. The empty space that I've gotten with him. Not empty in a bad way—but in a good way. Space that doesn't have to or need to be filled.

Just stillness and presence.

Victory.

However we write it and create it and let it play out.

Whatever you're battling, I encourage you to find space with it. Lean in and feel the breath of it. Find the heartbeat. Be present.

It's scary. I know. But so is chaotically running away or carelessly swinging your sword with no aim or direction.

And true, it may turn and destroy you.

It may break you.

But perhaps you've been put in this battle not to break—but to break open.

And maybe *that* is the victory?

Breathe in.

Breathe out.

Lean in.

I walked into the oncologist's office today to meet my dad for his chemo treatment.

The waiting room was packed with people who are battling cancer.

My first thought—

Fuck. That. Shit.

I know my ranting doesn't change anything.

But this is not okay.

My profanities are my outlet today.

Fuck.

That.

Shit.

I'm now sitting in a room of many many people who are hooked to IV pumps with chemo being administered.

One being my dad.

I feel like I'm on the battlefield right now with my hands tied behind my back. Just observing the war.

And that fucking pisses me off.

My dad is doing fine. He's eating Oreos. He's not coughing nearly as much. He just encouraged a guy sitting across the room from him. "You doing alright, partner? It's alright. I'm new to all this too, brother," he says.

I'm not pissed off that this is happening to him. I'm pissed that it's happening at all. Happening to anyone.

Individuals being ripped from their lives and shackled to their mortality.

It feels so wrong.

And there are so many people here today. Over 30. And that's just right here at this office. Today.

A young guy just walked in and is having his chemo drugs explained to him.

Cancer is inclusive.

Cancer gives no fucks.

You want to know the cool thing, though?

Community gets built when people are brought together with a centralized focus.

This community—they all want to live.

That is their focus.

The things that divide us don't seem to divide us in this room.

They don't seem separate here. They seem unified.

All battling. But all surviving.

The outcome—well, that's up in the air.

But they still showed up today.

Because that's what warriors do.

We all know the possible outcome of war. Not everyone will win. Just like in life. With life comes death. But the point of living is not to die. The point of living is to live.

Death is the ultimate outcome.

Whether now or later.

That's no shock or surprise.

Or it shouldn't be.

It's the battle that matters. It's the mindset that matters.

Keep your head in the game. Those were the surgeon's words to my dad when he told him he had Stage 4 Colorectal Cancer.

In other words—keep fighting. Keep showing up. Keep believing.

Battle on, Warrior.

Whatever you've got going on today that is hard—really hard. Keep standing. It ain't over. Don't back down. Don't give up. Don't lose sight of the victory.

In the words of my dad, "I ain't dead yet." And neither are you.

Battle on, Warrior.

In this room, right here—right now. Cancer gives zero fucks.

But neither do these Warriors.

They're all in.

Battling on.

Today is chemo day. It's when I really come face to face with the reality that my dad is battling cancer.

Things have been really good since his last chemo treatment—two weeks ago.

The chronic cough is almost completely gone. He's living life. He cut tree limbs the other day. He can talk without coughing in between breaths.

But today—we'll sit together for five hours while he gets his chemo infusion.

Chemo-Wednesday, in an odd way, is one of my favorite days with him.

It's so incredibly special. He handles it like a champ. It's just me and him and a room full of others who are battling cancer. The shock of cancer is losing its grip. Shock and awe fade. Because when it's time to fight—you fight.

When it's time to endure—you endure.

When it's time to stand—you stand.

Firm.

I'm so grateful for this time together. The circumstances, not so much.

Man, we can be a fickle people. But the challenges of life have a way of solidifying us.

When people ask me, 'How's your dad?' I answer with, 'He's good'"

When people ask me, 'How are you?' I answer with, 'I'm grateful.'

Because I am.

Truly.

Glory!

I'm holding a doctor's note that says my dad is handling treatment well and can return to work!

Hell. Yeah.

My dad finished his fourth chemo treatment this week.

He's back at work at about 85–90% of *himself*. He said most days he does well, but after chemo this week he was pretty tired.

The chronic cough is gone.

In two weeks he'll go for a CT scan to see if the chemo is working. Our family is very eager for this appointment.

I told my dad that his journey has really rescripted my mind around cancer.

I think we often hear *cancer* and immediately think—*either cure it or die from it*. And yes, this is definitely a reality of cancer. However, we don't often think of *managing cancer* just as you would high blood pressure or high cholesterol.

Those things can kill suddenly—and so can cancer. But those things can also be managed—so can cancer.

My dad told me he figured he'd just die of a stroke or heart attack one day.

I'm so glad that wasn't the case and that it's *just* cancer.

Whether I had gotten 24 hours with him or 24 more days—it sure would have beat a sudden loss.

To be here 90 days later is a gift.

Such a gift.

Cancer is shitty, and I hate it. But it's just like every other disease that snatches life from us.

With my dad, this journey has taught me not to focus on death.

That's inevitable.

But to focus on life.

And that's what we continue to do.

Death is certainly promised to all of us at some point on this journey.

But life isn't.

To live life—a thriving life. Now, that's a choice. That's intentional.

This cancer diagnosis woke my dad up to his life.

He's now living his life.

Awake.

Living.

Should you find yourself in a place where you're waking up to new ideas and concepts—and your first thought is *my family and community would never understand or accept this.*

I can assure you that you're onto something grand.

Most likely the ticket to your freedom.

If you're moved. Excited. Feel like you can breathe for the first time in a long time—if not the first time ever—

you've probably woken up to your truth.

Or a piece of it.

Anxiety chases the initial revelation of truth.

It's scary.

Truth asks you to return to yourself. To your nature. To your creativity.

Through the lens of Truth, you're no longer small. Or weak. Or fragile.

You're bold. Courageous. Powerful.

Love abounds where Truth resides.

So, if you're relieved by this new thought but also trembling because of what others are going to say or think—you're on the right path.

Fear is just part of it.

People may get mad. They may reject. They may even leave your side.

That's okay.

You'll be okay.

Light and dark will always be intertwined. That's not a bad thing. It's neither good nor bad. It just is.

The shadow has its place.

On my journey—it ultimately catapulted me to where I needed to be.

Where Love abounds. Recklessly.

Stop resisting, Truth-seeker.

Maybe the anxiety is not a sign you're going the wrong direction. Maybe it's a gravitational pull—letting you know you're on the right path.

You are who you're looking for. You've got the answer.

Freedom is in the mystery. Oftentimes—on the other side of the anxiety.

Wake up, O' sleeper and rise.

Lean in.

Great appointment today!

My dad had scans done yesterday and received results today. His lymph nodes are healing and treatment is working.

He's doing so good.
Today was a good day. A very good day.
My soul, it is well.

Gratitude:

The quality of being thankful; readiness to show appreciation for and to return kindness.

I feel an overwhelming urge to continuously bring attention to the time that we have together. We celebrated Thanksgiving with my family today.

Although the seat at the table is always promised—the *person* who sits in that chair is not.

Yet, here we are—another year with everyone taking their seat at the table.

There will come a day when a seat or two are empty. But for today, for this Thanksgiving—those seats were all full.

Full.

And so is my belly.

And so is my heart.

I can't help but point out that my dad sat at his spot at the table this year. Just like he does every year. I was more attentive to him sitting there than I ever have been.

His taste buds aren't the same—but he's still here.

Four months since his diagnosis.

Time is warped sometimes.

What seems like an eternity has only been four months. Yet I'm so grateful for these four months. I'm grateful for the moments. The sweetest, raw, most tender moments.

The beauty of light and dark colliding. Just like the sunrise. Just like the sunset. Like the dimension of art—shadows and light moving together to make beauty. To bring depth.

Cancer is fighting for my dad's life. But my dad is fighting for his life as well. And that's one person I wouldn't want to be up against.

At this time, my dad is winning.

In one breath I'm so fucking angry at the fact my dad has cancer. But in another, I find myself grateful for this season. I cry when I write this. Because I want to hate every bit of it. But cancer has given more life to my dad in these past four months than he had prior to his diagnosis.

This gave him a spark. A path. A renewed purpose and passion. Cancer, if the goal was to show up to bring death—you don't win. Because your presence—it brought life.

It brought life to my dad and to all who are around him.

You gave us a reminder that the seats are not promised to be full every year.

And for that…. Even for you…. I'm finding gratitude.

I've still got my dad.

And the seats were still full.

I hope you enjoy the full seats at your table. And if a seat or two are empty, I hope you take time to feel and grieve—and make time to enjoy the seats that are still occupied.

It's a gift.

Life is a gift.

I'm thankful.

I've had people tell me I am wise.

They compliment my ability to set firm boundaries.

They applaud me for being sure of who I am and being clear about what I want.

It's an honor to be told I'm the *people whisperer* and that I bring good energy that changes the mood of the room.

Or that I'm respected because I'll say *no* and speak up when a voice needs to be heard.

I'm not one to turn down a good compliment. Words are my love language, and I'll soak 'em up—when they're genuine.

You're only seeing this version of me because of what I've been through.

I cannot tell you how deeply I hurt at times.

I can't even begin to give words to how much sorrow I have experienced.

The worst types of betrayals.

Gut wrenching.

Wrongfully accused.

Misunderstood.

Taken advantage of.

Treated unfairly.

I don't often talk about how many times I've screamed and cried to let the pain escape me.

Because there's a time to heal with others, and there's a time to heal alone.

I heal alone, a lot.

So, you don't see that part. Or hear about it.

No one sees the constant dying of myself and putting my ego in its place and how often I create grace for people's bullshit— including my own.

How often I make room for pain to sit with me

be poured on me

or burn me alive.

I continuously choose to walk back into the flames of humanity. Even with the risk of being burned.

Because we are a beautiful people.

And the beauty outweighs the pain for me.

Our complexities are a work of art.

Yes. Even the pain.

Hurt people hurt people. Scarcity creates fear, and fear makes us harm one another.

Insecurity makes people protect themselves at the expense of others.

I have my own pain.

My own sorrow.

My own tears that sneak up on me from time to time.

And a heart that breaks.

It is the breaking that keeps me human.

It is the breaking that keeps me curious.

It is the breaking that keeps me free.
It is the breaking that keeps me healing.
Every time my heart breaks—
I actively choose to open it up again. The breaking creates complexities. But it also creates a fresh new space.
If you let it.
It might seem like some selfless act.
It's not.
I don't do it for you.
I do it for me.
I stay human for me.
I stay curious for me.
I stay free for me.
I heal for me.
And somehow that pours out of me and back into humanity.
Free for the taking—if one might want it.
We all have our own stories filled with traumas and heartbreaks.
Every single one of us.
We all have a choice for what we do with those traumas and heartbreaks.
You can't control what happened to you.
You can control your attitude. You can control your actions. You can control how you decide to heal.
If you want to heal.
You can pick up the broken pieces around you and decide what you want to do next with them.
My unsolicited advice?
Heal.
Do it for you.
Whatever that looks like.
So that we can all continue to partake from the stream of humanity with all its beautiful complications.
Don't stop the flow.
The goal is not to avoid pain.
Pain is inevitable.
The goal is to keep healing.

Keep making room.
Keep creating space.
Do it for you.
Do it
for
you.

My dad completed his sixth chemo treatment this week.

He's doing well.

The building up of chemo is tiring his body—but the cancer is losing at this point.

Keep going, dad. You got this.

My dad. A grown man, sitting on his legs, on the floor across from my baby boy.

The pictures and videos I captured of these moments today make tears rush to my eyes, and I'm grateful to have them to look back on.

Sway and Papa hung out on the floor of Sway's bedroom for half an hour.

Laughing. Talking. Making car sounds as they pushed Hot Wheels around the room.

It was magical.

Children playing.

I watch my dad in moments like this as if I'm seeing a story unfold. It's like he knows something we don't know.

He's taking time without rushing. He's taking it all in.

The disease of apathy is far more fatal than a cancer diagnosis.

The cancer diagnosis brought my dad back to life.

It brought our relationship back to life.

This week he'll endure chemo treatment number seven, and I'll be there right beside him.

Chemo is taking its toll. But my dad will keep fighting.

And I'll keep fighting beside him. Until he wins or says he's done. Either way—I'm along for the journey.

"Whoever humbles himself like this child is the greatest in the kingdom of heaven."

~Jesus

"Pearl. Just takin' it one day at a time. That's all we ever had anyway."

~My dad

Chemo Infusion Number Seven—down.

I had to pull over on my way home this afternoon to take in a magical view of the sun setting.

Right after my dad had surgery and wasn't bouncing back, we thought it was over for him. He thought it was over for him.

His oncologist, Dr. Murphy, had shared with him that his cancer was terminal. But no one knew that except my dad—and now me.

He and I sat on his couch and talked about life and death.

He wept.

So did I.

Thirty-four years and I never even saw his eyes get teary. But that day he broke down.

I jumped in his lap and hugged him.

We had just finished a conversation about light and dark colliding. How they make beauty together.

As I hugged him, through the tears I said, "You'll always be with me. I'll carry you with me always. And I'll always see you in the beauty of light and darkness—in the sunrise. In the sunset. You'll be there."

The beauty of this sunset I'm gazing upon is simply the beauty of this moment.

My dad is still here. I don't need to see him in the sunset because I actually just saw him.

Whatever you've got going on, friend—just take it one day at a time. That's all we ever have anyway.

There will be beauty from the ashes. There always is. There always will be.

I watched you tonight.
You were taking in the moments.
You were present.
Soaking it all up.
I watched you tonight.
Celebrating Christmas like you never have before.
As if it were your last.
I watched you laugh and talk and eat.
Celebrate with all you have.
I watched you love—unconditionally.
I watched you grow tired and fatigued... and yet you hung around for the party. You stayed in the center of the party.
I watched you live.
In your suffering you are teaching us how to live.
Thank you for enduring the battle, Dad.
Tonight was pure joy and you led the way.

"Train yourself to let go of everything you fear to lose."
~Yoda

2019, I celebrate you. I applaud you.
You were really my first full year of freedom.
The result and reward of many years of finding myself and stepping into all that I am—or know that I am as of now.
Free from the expectations of others.
Free from the burden of an ideology that winds up being a torture chamber of shame and guilt.
Free from carrying the weight of what others may think.

2019 was when I found my footing.
I discovered my edge.
I anchored to the trust in me.
In my ability to lead the way and find the answers for myself.
I experienced the deepest, gut-wrenching heartache I've ever experienced.
Abruptly slammed into the reality that my dad has cancer.
Watching him endure a couple of months facing death.
Watching death literally take him away.
One shallow breath at a time.
And yet he bounced back.
Almost six months heavy in battle.
Winning.
Chemo treatment number eight is on deck—next week. I've never experienced anything more real in my life.
I preach about leaning in. This year, I had an opportunity to live it out—and am still living it out—leaning in.
2019 has been lovely. A great year. A safe place to lay my head for a bit. A haven where I stepped into my gifts as an empath. Discovered my heart on a deeper spiritual level than I ever have.
A year when I embraced my husband and my children more than I ever have.
Understanding life is fleeting.
Not in fear—but in awe.
2019. I applaud you. I thank you. I'm grateful for the time we had.
2020—I welcome you with arms wide open.
Leaning in.
Loving big.
Living free.

Chemo treatment number nine is well underway.
Dad had his second set of scans today since starting chemo.
Treatment. Is. Working.
What else can I say?

As my dad's surgeon said after removing his tumor and diagnosing him with stage 4 cancer—*Today is a good day. And if today is good, I'm hopeful tomorrow will be good too.*

Today is a good day. Here's to tomorrow.

*Five minutes after I wrote this my dad had an allergic reaction to the chemo drug.

The medical staff gave him Benadryl and backed him off that particular chemo. They said they have seen this happen before in other patients. The body starts to reject the chemotherapy. My dad has to shift directions with his treatment plan. His body will no longer tolerate this one.

I've watched people change.

Whether by circumstance. Or money. Or power. Personal gain. Position. Or Fear.

They change.

I've watched the most loyal fold for their own safety and survival.

I've watched the behaviors around people-pleasing and survival mode.

We often claim, "I would never..." but when you're facing the fire? Then what?

To watch people throw others out as a means of deflection... or save themselves over their tribe.

That is not honorable.

It will never be honorable.

We all know what it feels like for someone to stand with us or stand against us.

Just know, when it comes down to it, whether right or wrong, people will most likely choose themselves first. They will protect and save themselves first.

And I don't fault them for this.

It's what we're wired to do.

Save yourself. Get personal gain for yourself. Take care of you. At all costs.

Basic survival.

It's not shocking anymore. It just is.

The pain, the betrayal—it's inevitable.

Letting it break you, harden you, make you fall into a victim mindset or make you resentful and angry... well, that's a choice.

Keep choosing to fight for the good of humanity.

It's multifaceted and complicated.

If you're wired to, stand for those who can't stand and speak for those with no voice. Keep on keepin' on.

Don't let those who are fearful, out for personal gain due to control and survival destroy you—or your heart.

Keep loving. Keep on loving.

Your reward is coming.

Anyone who tells you to run from the darkness—run away from *them*.

The running away from darkness is what keeps you in a state of anxiety.

The running away is what keeps you feeling like you're missing something.

You have everything you need for wholeness—but if you forsake your darkness, you are incomplete.

The darkness is not bad. It's just you.

And you are not bad.

Who you are is not bad.

Sit with it.

Listen to it.

Embrace it.

Apologize to yourself for labeling a part of you as bad, and then reshape it.

Mold it.

Direct it.

But whatever you do—don't run from it.

You are lovable. You are worthy. You are deserving.

You—the light and the dark in you.
All of you.

～

"Awareness is like the sun. When it shines on things, they are transformed."

~Thich Nhat Hanh

～

Chemo treatment #10 of 12 (we hope) in the books.
Six months since my dad's cancer diagnosis.
Things are going really well.
I'm just very weepy today.
Tired. Overwhelmed. Exhausted.
I'm tired of seeing people fight each other because of skewed perspectives.
I'm tired of witnessing people's egos block them from the abundance they deserve.
Defensiveness.
It makes me sick watching people continuously defend and waste their precious energy on resisting instead of learning to let go.
To trust.
To free flow.
As if our resistance, defensiveness, or ego has ever positioned us in a better place.
If we could only move out of our own way.
If we'd just stop blaming others and start looking within—we'd see we are our own worst enemies.
Not them.
We cause our setbacks.
Not them.
No one can take what belongs to you. No one.
The need to control. To tear others down. To gossip. To spew negativity.

This is how people are choosing to spend the precious time in their life.

Next week my dad will celebrate his 54th birthday.

A few months ago we didn't even think we'd get another opportunity to celebrate another year of his life.

Wake up people.

Shut up.

Stop all the noise.

Shut the hell up.

Make your life worth living.

Trust me. It's fleeting.

It's fleeting.

Stop blaming others. Stop talking about others. Stop complaining and recklessly spewing words with damaging energy.

Start talking to each other directly and try to work it out.

Partner together with the people around you.

Not everyone is out to get you or take from you.

Get over yourself and get out of your way—and live.

I'm begging you.

D_{ad.}

Happy 54th birthday to you.

Thank you for fighting to live.

Thank you for still being here.

You mask your pain. You don't speak of your struggle very often. So, it's easy to think you're okay.

And that things are normal.

I thought we were going to lose you at 53 years old.

But here you are. 54 today.

You've got more life to live.

Keep pressing forward.

Happy Birthday!

My family celebrated my dad big tonight.
By "big," I mean we slowed down.
We drank. We ate. We laughed over the stupidest things.
Like, belly-laughed.
Laughed so hard, we couldn't breathe.
Pressed pause.
Captured a moment in time.
Because we all realize just how thin the veil is between this life and what's next.
Happy 54th birthday to my dad!
There was a moment where even the most optimistic of us didn't think you'd see 54.
But here you are.
Here we are.
Funny how I'm just learning what *family* truly means. I had to let go of expectations and the imagery of what I thought it *should* be.
That took a lot of years.
Forgiveness. Grace. Patience. Growth. Maturity. Healing. And ultimately just choosing to love the people around me without an agenda.
The realization that I am not my parents or what I perceive as their shortcomings.
And learning to love them right where they are—as they are.
That's family.
Creating boundaries and pulling away so you can heal.
Healing.
Then moving close again.
The ebb and flow of relationship and all that it entails.
Family.
I'm glad I didn't give up on y'all.
I'm glad y'all didn't give up on me.
I'm glad we have these moments still.
My soul—it is well.

Treatment went well today.

Dad and his oncologist even discussed the possibility of a reversal on his colostomy in the near future.

However, I can't help but sit here with this overwhelming bittersweet feeling.

We were celebrating the completion of treatment #11 in hopes that #12 was his last, and he'd be ringing the bell in two weeks—ringing the bell is the celebratory "I'm done" moment.

We inquired about his last treatment, big smiles on our faces, and to our surprise the doctor said:

"You'll never be done."

We stood there, stunned.

The doctor went on to explain that my dad is doing really well, and he's now in "maintenance."

Which is great. But with his type and stage of cancer, he's never going to be *done*.

Treatment may take on new forms as time goes on—but it will always be part of his life going forward.

My dad just stood there and took that news.

His response—

"I'ma do whatever the hell you tell me to do, Doc."

My dad is a warrior.

He doesn't get caught up in his headspace. He straight up told me during a past conversation that he doesn't understand how people have anxiety. *Why give your head that much power over things that aren't real?*

That's what he told me.

You just go with what ya got... and fight for what ya want.

The simplicity baffles me.

As of now, there is no end in sight.

We are adjusting our focus. And by "we"... I mean *me*.

Victory is complex. It's not like the movies.

I'll leave you with this quote that my daughter, Trinity's track coach, said this afternoon when I picked her up from practice. It's very fitting for this moment.

"We are gonna be champions in our own minds first, and then we'll let the body catch up."

Coach Humphrey's words were timely.

Very timely.

*Since referencing Coach Humphrey's words, Coach Humphery actually passed away from cancer. Just as I shared in the eulogy about the author Jim Butcher, our words and creativity are gifts we release. It takes on an energy of its own once we part from it. Coach Humphrey's words are still moving beyond his physical presence here on earth. They moved from him, to his track team, to me—a parent sitting among the team, to this book and now to you.

I'm not thrilled about being at the dentist.

Actually, dentist visits bring up excruciating anxiety for me.

The noises, the feelings, your mouth cranked open, just all the weird and uncomfortable stuff.

And even though all of that can bring on anxiety... it's actually performance anxiety that takes over.

It's bizarre.

I've always had performance anxiety when it comes to doctors and such. I was taught as a kid that the doctors are here to help and the appointment will be less painful if I listen and obey.

So, I do.

And even though this dentist really is helping me, I still can't help but want to scream, cry, and run away.

It's what my body wants to do.

Because my mind whispers, "You are incapable."

Don't ask me why. I'm not sure why I feel "incapable" at the dentist.

But I get this daunting feeling that I'm stuck. Trapped. Or something bad will happen.

I know those thoughts are not real.

But my nervous system and body say otherwise.

I don't scream. I don't cry. I don't run away.

I lie here and trust the process.

I talk myself through it one breath at a time.

I tell myself a new story in my mind—"You're okay. This will not last forever. You've gotten through a dentist visit before and you'll get through it again. You are safe here. Keep breathing. It's okay that you're feeling afraid. Be afraid if you need to—but keep breathing."

You see, there is something magical about learning to trust yourself. You learn to champion yourself. I've learned to coach myself through difficult moments. But I only listen because I trust the voice that is speaking to me.

My own voice.

You can do hard things. You are stronger than you give yourself credit for.

Your life story carries a theme of overcoming, and yet you still doubt yourself.

Why?

We're not running from being human anymore.

We're not white-knuckling life. We're just living. Right?

Waves of anxiety will always find a way to wash upon us. And that's okay. It's what you do with that anxiety—

Do you absorb it, believe it, fall under its spell?

Or do you acknowledge it and let it freely flow in and out?

Anxiety is not meant to be the final outcome.

Anxiety just is.

Just like our breath.

You don't breathe to hold your breath.

You breathe to inhale and exhale.

To move with the breath.

To live.

To be human.

Anxiety is something you move with.

It means you're living. It means you're human.

We just need to wrap our arms around ourselves and remind ourselves that we are human.

Even when you revert back to a five-year-old child in the dental chair. You're still human.

You're still growing.

You're still overcoming.

You're still trusting.

Lean in.

This is 35.

Strong—inside and outside.

Confident.

Gentle. Yet firm.

I've never loved myself or trusted myself more.

I've never loved or trusted others more.

Two years ago I left a lot behind. Including the bondage of a belief system that made guilt and shame a virtue.

When I stopped apologizing for being me, transformation happened.

I stopped playing small.

Don't you dare play small so that others feel more confident. Not your place, my friend.

Show up strong when you're strong.

Show up shattered when you're shattered.

It's called being human.

Stop making excuses for being human and just *be*.

Stop apologizing and just *be*.

Stop drowning in shame and guilt and excuses about why you're not enough and just *be*.

You are enough.

You are whole.

You are complete.

There is nothing *out there* that will save you.

Nothing *out there* has your answer.

Nothing *out there* holds your happiness.

You have it all.

But you believe otherwise.

I've made it to 35 years old, and I don't take that lightly.

I don't want you to contribute to a charity for my birthday. I don't need gifts—or even words of affirmation.

My birthday wish is that *you* would wake up to your power this year.

My wish is that *you* would stop being controlled by fear and lean in instead.

You carry strength—you just need to show up and take hold of it.

"You only are free when you realize you belong no place — you belong every place—no place at all. The price is high. The reward is great."

~Maya Angelou

Today is Chemo Wednesday.

Visitors weren't allowed because of the outbreak of CoronaVirus.

I don't know which number this was. I stopped counting once we found out there is no end to chemo for dad.

Counting chemo treatments when you're counting down is motivating. But counting them just to be counting them is torture.

My dad called me after chemo. We talked for a couple hours just like we would if I was sitting beside him during his infusion.

He shared that his lymph nodes still look good, but something in the blood test—I'm always trying to decipher his version of what he heard from the doctor, so bear with me—is *high* and leading them to believe the cancer may be spreading. Not sure yet. More tests next time.

He sounded a little bummed and tired as he shared with me that he's going to have to continue chemo every two weeks indefinitely. *Indefinitely.*

At a previous appointment his oncologist said he might be able to switch over to a new treatment plan that wouldn't include such frequent chemo infusions.

But that wasn't the case anymore.

Which led us to navigate the depths of a conversation no one wants to have.

Death.

We've had quite a few of those throughout this cancer journey. But not recently.

"This really isn't about saving you at this point, huh? It's just about extending your life with quality while you journey home?" I asked.

"Yup." He responded.

Neither of us emotional or sad. Just talking. As if we were discussing the weather.

"How are you feeling? Do you feel *it* approaching or getting close?" I asked.

"My body is getting tired, Pearl," he said

Today is one of those days where you feel the shadow. But shadows don't exist without light.

My dad is still working at his job. No plans of stopping. Even with a global pandemic and a compromised immune system, he says in his stubborn, country accent, "Ah, I ain't gonna stop working—that just is what it is."

To which I laugh and say, "Dad! I didn't expect any different from you. You're the type that will fight for your life but also accept your fate. You sat at home for far too long in the beginning of this journey, I can't imagine a deadly (to you) virus making you sit down somewhere. That would just be too easy."

He laughed.

Then we carried on with conversations about other topics.

Another day, friends.

Even with the shadows lurking—we're still walking in light. Hand in hand—even with social distancing. Heart to heart—even though our hearts are aching.

We don't deny the shadows that are drawing closer. We acknowledge them. Finding a sense of gratitude for their presence. A respect of sorts … but for today—we keep pressing forward in light.

Today.

That's all we ever really have anyway.

"Try to imagine what it will be like to go to sleep and never wake up. Now try to imagine what it was like to wake up having never gone to sleep."

~Alan Watts

I'm going to paraphrase something profound my friend, Andrea, shared with me the other day:

> *Times like this—people have historically become more of what they already are and less of what they have pretended to be.*
> *Those who pay attention have a magnifying glass to all of it.*
> *Usually those people are the empathetic ones.*
> *They become better because they pay attention.*
> *They change their mindsets, routines, and eliminate the people who steal their peace.*
> *Bad people become worse.*
> *Greedy people become greedier.*
> *But humanity will show clearer.*
> *The helpers will spring forth. The selfless will spring forth.*
> *Those types of people rise during times like these.*

Are you rising?

Taught my dad how to do a video call, since I can't be with him at chemo because of the pandemic.

He video-called me on the way home from the clinic.

They didn't do any treatment today. According to his blood-work, he needs new medications. The current treatment plan doesn't seem to be working anymore.

Not for this aggressive cancer.

He'll go back for treatment next week, new medication, new plan.

We are merely moving shadows.

All of us.

Overcast of darkness but still reflecting light.

Sometimes you laugh.

Sometimes you cry.

Sometimes you laugh to keep from crying.

And sometimes you do both simultaneously.

Today, we laughed. Still.

But tonight, in my reflection of the day, I weep.

Mostly grateful tears. But also mixed with empathy that he's going through this and most likely, this will be the battle that takes him from this earth.

Ultimately.

At some point.

Whether the end is near or far, Dad... damn, we're writing a good story in the meantime.

Lean in, Warrior.

And to those who read this amidst your own battles—

Lean in, Warriors. Battle on.

I took a drive this evening.

By myself.

Just chasing the sunset like I did prior to the world's abrupt halt because of this pandemic.

It's what I did a lot last summer after the news of my dad's diagnosis with cancer.

Chased the sunset.

Embracing the beauty of the light against the darkness.

It's been about four weeks since my dad received his last chemo. He's supposed to get an infusion every two weeks.

His medicine is being altered, and there's been a hold up. He's coughing again. Just like he did back in the beginning.

Slowly suffocating on tumor fluid and hoping this new treatment brings relief.

"What are your thoughts, Dad?" I asked him today.

"Keep going as long as I can, April. That's all I can do."

His head is still in the game.

He's still fighting.

He's still living.

And I'm still chasing the sunset. Being reminded of my dad in the progression of the sunset—even though he's still physically here.

I'm grateful he's still physically here.

Dad, I won't stop you from going where you need to go. But thank you for holding on a little longer.

Hold on just a little longer.

A friend of mine lost her dad abruptly last week.

It was unexpected.

When I reached out to offer my condolences she gave me a piece of advice for my journey with my own dad.

She said, "Ask him as many questions as you can while you have the time."

I heed that advice.

Today I asked my dad why he named me April.

Apparently when I was born there was a debacle between him and my mom over my name.

She wanted Amber. He wanted April.

There's always a story behind a name being chosen, so I asked him why April—thinking there would be some beautiful story to follow.

This was his response:

"There was an April and an Amber when I was in school. One was an ugly bitch, and the other was a pretty blonde ... so there you go. There wasn't any way in hell you were going to be named Amber."

I laughed for at least 20 minutes after he shared this with me.

No beautiful story.

Just his raw honesty.

Just my dad being my dad.

Right now I'm hanging my head in tears.

My dad had chemo today for the first time in six weeks.

He was supposed to go last week—but his new medicine still hadn't arrived.

Today, he got an infusion.

I just spent the last hour talking to him.

I cried.

He goes—"Now, don't you go getting all emotional on me, Pearl."

I jokingly begged him not to die during this time of the pandemic. Because if he does—I can't be with him or attend his funeral... being the highlight of his funeral.

He laughed. He agreed he wouldn't go yet.

He said, "If it wasn't for you kids and your mama—I wouldn't have done all this."

He's in bad shape.

But it ain't over till it's over.

And today—it ain't over.

Not quite yet.

I watched the sunset while talking to him this evening.

The sun is still setting. The birds are still chirping.

My dad—he's still living. Still breathing. Still pressing forward.

I know there will come a day when I post about his homecoming...

But that is not today.

Not today.

Today we lean in.

No matter how much we try to cling to a moment. It is only a moment. It flees.

The shadow moves closer.

It always will.

Life is not about avoiding the shadow or running far from it.

Life is about embracing the shadow. Letting it move in as it

naturally does. Absorbing the sun till the last drop. And leaning
in with radical acceptance toward the things we cannot change.
Sometimes as darkness moves in, beauty comes with it.
We will miss the beauty if we are in a place of avoidance.
Denial.
Resistance.
This is a rollercoaster, and I refuse to close my eyes.
I'm choosing to keep my eyes open.
If I shut the bad out, I shut the good out too.
I want to see it all.
Feel it all.
All of it.
This is living.
Whoever programmed you for a fairytale ending. Fuck them.
That's not real.
This is real.
You are real.
Light and darkness colliding are real.
Shadows are real.
Beauty from ashes—that's real.
May we cling to what is real. Moving with life.
See it all.
Feel it all.
Choose to keep our eyes open.
And keep leaning in.

D ad.
Hang on.
Please hang on.

I haven't seen my dad in three months due to the pandemic and
all the unknown.

But I saw him today.

He's okay...

...ish.

This cough is the worst. It's tiring him out.

He can't talk without coughing. He can't lay back or lie down without coughing, so he sits straight up and very still.

Five weeks of coughing like this, and he's strained something in his stomach and groin.

It's awful.

Sadly, it's not *just* a cough. The cancer is in his lymph nodes that line his trachea. It's inflamed and causes bronchial spasms.

It's constant.

I'm glad I get to see him face to face.

Even though the circumstances aren't ideal—I'm seeing him face to face.

Question everything you've been taught to believe.

Differentiate between your thoughts and *their* thoughts.

Your inner voice is hidden under the rubbish of modern culture, your childhood fears of not belonging, your parents' expectations, and all the other boxes that the world told you to fit inside.

Question everything.

Question your habits.

Question what makes you mad—and *why* it makes you mad.

Question your behaviors.

Your responses.

Your fight or flight reactions.

Your survival skills.

Question your judgments.

What you despise—question *why* you despise it so much.

Question ideologies.

Beliefs.

Traditions.

Question it all until you hear yourself thinking.

When you hear your unfiltered voice, you may feel you're on the edge of going crazy.
What if you're not going crazy?
What if you're just waking up?
Question everything.
The truth you are seeking is seeking you.

Chased down the sunset this evening.
There's just something about trying to hang on a little longer to something beautiful that's fleeting.
Slipping from your grasp.
But not quite gone yet.
Darkness closing in from behind. Eclipsing what was once light. Moving swiftly.
It doesn't wait.
No matter how hard you resist or press against it—you'll get swallowed up too.
So, I don't spend my days fighting the darkness anymore.
I try to position myself somewhere between the darkness and the light.
Dark on one side.
Light on the other.
And if possible, me in the middle.
It's from this angle that we capture the beauty.
It's where we feel most alive.
Most free.
It's where we can catch a breath.
It's where we can just be.
The noise of this world falls away for this brief moment.
Your heart is speaking.
Your breath is speaking.
The sky is speaking.
The wind is speaking.
The earth cries out.... And you stop to listen.

To take it all in.
Whatever mountains you're facing—they will not overtake you.
They're yours.
You own them.
You speak to them and tell them to move.
You hold that power.
Or maybe—just maybe you let them be.
Maybe the mountain is sheltering you.
What you think is an obstacle is actually a covering.
Protection.
Either way, this is your story.
Your journey.
You don't have to choose to stand with light or dark.
You can choose to stand in between.
You can choose to watch the light show.
We can grieve all the way to our bones and still enjoy the journey.
I'm grateful for the journey.
For another sunset.
For the option to choose to continue to love.
Knowing it comes with the risk of great loss.
Knowing love is worth it.
Keep choosing love.
Keep chasing sunsets.
Hold your ground in the middle and don't close your eyes.
Prepare for the best views.

The oncologist's office called while my dad was getting chemo.
His breathing is not sufficient.
They said he needs to go to the hospital.
My mom and I met at the oncologist office, and an ambulance was waiting.
Apparently my dad requested the ambulance.
I did see him briefly when the EMTs brought him out on the stretcher.

No one can go to the hospital due to safety measures because of the pandemic

So, we wait for an update.

He texted my mom a few minutes ago and said, "This is going to be fun." So—we assume he's on some good meds.

Oh, Dad.

Keep clinging.

Yesterday was rough. He had his scheduled chemo and a routine CT scan. After the doctor reviewed the scans, he saw the new treatment hasn't been working at all. So, basically six weeks on this new treatment has been like being with no treatment. They canceled treatment for the day and asked him to come back today for a new plan.

This cancer is nasty, and it wants the lungs.

The right side of my dad's body has been swollen for a while. His doctor said he thinks it's from the inflammation in his lymph nodes. But he wanted him to go for some scans on his leg to make sure it's not a blood clot.

When my mom and dad got to the imaging office, my dad went to the bathroom. My mom said he didn't come back out, so she was concerned.

She could hear him coughing. He finally came out—white and clammy.

She asked, "Are you okay?" As she walked towards him, he fell to his knees at her feet and started coughing up blood.

He looked up at her and said through his panting breath, "I think I'm dying."

She yelled, "*No you're not!*"

A swarm of nurses ran over to care for him.

They got his breathing under control and asked if he wanted to go to the hospital. He said no—of course. A nurse called his oncologist, and Dr. Murphy said that coughing up blood is a side effect to the chemo he was on.

They finished the scans, and my dad went home.

Today, he showed up for the new chemo. It was successfully administered—but they couldn't send him home with his lack of oxygen. So, they told him he was going to be admitted to the hospital.

Give his body a break. Get his breathing back in line.

He didn't object and requested an ambulance.

I saw him as they pushed him out on the stretcher. I had two seconds to speak to him. He sternly told me to call his boss, Tracy, and give him an update.

The last I heard from my dad via text, he's still in the ER. They've done CT scans. He's hot, and he's hungry. And he can't see shit past the mask they have over his face.

His words, not mine.

Cling, Dad. Hold onto your life and don't let up. You've got a lot of people championing you.

For now, we wait.

We lean in.

We keep leaning in.

A few weeks ago I went to the mailbox and found a card that was sent to me by my friend Christina. It was right on time.

On the front a picture of me with my mom, dad, and brothers. With the words, "Good vibes."

Good vibes.

It gave me good vibes even when things are severely shitty.

I just spoke to a nurse at the hospital.

The nurse was really kind. Here is the update she gave me:

My dad was admitted to the Critical Care Unit.

He has pneumonia and a PE in the upper lobe—Pulmonary embolism (PE) is when a blood clot (thrombus) becomes lodged in an artery in the lung and blocks blood flow to the lung. They are giving him medicine to thin his blood and dissolve the blood clot.

He's on oxygen.

He's awake and alert. He's in good spirits.

He's still coughing, and they are trying to keep him as comfortable as they can. The nurse said he'll continue to cough for the next day or so, and then it will start to get better.

Tomorrow his oncologist and pulmonologist will visit him and come up with a game plan.

He is allowed to have visitors, one at a time, in 15–30 minute increments.

It sounds like my mom and my dad will get to sleep tonight for the first time in months.

Good vibes.

Keep sending good vibes.

It ain't over yet.

James, my dad's nurse in the Critical Care Unit, let me break the rules.

He didn't limit me to 30 minutes. I stayed with my dad for hours.

He was talking in full sentences for quite a while. Only a few coughing spasms in the beginning and some pretty bad spasms before I left for the evening. Which is normal in the evenings.

He's coughing up some blood, but James says this is normal with my dad's situation, and we want him to keep clearing out his lungs.

They served my dad pot roast, mashed potatoes, and green beans. He was looking forward to this meal.

Unfortunately, chemo has ruined his taste, and he didn't like the pot roast.

So, I ate it and told him it was awful—the most disgusting thing I've ever eaten... (it was delicious).

We had a good time. We talked about life. Death. Dying fast. Dying slow.

He said, "I'm dying slowly."

I said, "So am I. We all are."

He nodded in agreement.

Then I said, "Dad—we know this cancer is going to move to

your lungs. We know this. And if it's there now, that doesn't mean you're dead today."

Earlier the pulmonologist told him they need to do a biopsy on his lungs to confirm what's going on with them, but they'll wait until next week when some of this infection is gone.

I told him, "Listen. First step—clear up pneumonia. Get you breathing. Then, we get you up walking. Then, we get you living life again—and we get you back to work. How's that sound?"

He nodded in agreement. "I ain't dead yet, Pearl."

True, Dad.

You sure ain't.

I t's hard as hell to see my dad like this. But—I'm grateful he's in a place where he can get back up on his feet.

He just has to *want* to get back on his feet.

And that's his choice.

Because this is his battle.

I wholeheartedly believe he can get back up and even get back to work.

I don't believe this is over.

Will you believe with me?

Will you intervene and believe for my dad in his unbelief?

I told my dad since he's confined to his bed with nothing better to do—he has to read my first published book.

It's very fitting since the title is *Pressing Forward*.

That's exactly what he's going to do—keep pressing forward.

Not as many coughing spasms today. He's still having them, but not like he was yesterday.

And he's in a way better mood. He's talking about "when" he leaves the hospital.

Tonight, for dinner he had turkey with gravy, mashed potatoes, and green beans. Meat makes him want to throw up. He said he can't taste it, and the texture is terrible.

One bite of the turkey and he said, "Nope. You can eat that, Pearl." And I ate it.

And it was delicious—I mean, horribly disgusting—or at least that's what I told him.

I leave you with this amazing quote from today:

> *"I'm gonna be really pissed off if I can't eat meat anymore.*
> *Because being a vegan is not something I call cool."*
>
> ~William Dotson

I wanted to sleep in this morning but woke up at 8:39 AM.

My phone was ringing. "Dad" on the screen.

I answered expecting him to be picking with me. I haven't heard from him on the phone in quite a while. I figured he was feeling better, able to talk, and that's why he was calling.

He could talk well.

He said, "Pearl, I need you down here by 1:00 to talk to the doctor."

My response—"Okay. Why?"

His response—"They want to know how I want to die."

I rushed to the hospital to get more details. My dad doesn't always hear all the details, so I wanted to hear for myself.

My mom met me there. The hospital doctor shared with us the risks of performing a biopsy.

Especially in Dad's condition.

She explained that my dad has some heart failure in two parts of his heart. He also has an obstruction in his abdomen that is hindering proper circulation to his right leg.

She said the cancer looks to be spreading all throughout his lungs, but they cannot confirm without a biopsy.

However, the biopsy has significant risks. She asked us if my dad died during the procedure, do we want them to resuscitate?

She shared how hard CPR is on the body and that he'd be ventilated if CPR was successful.

Hospital policy is to leave him that way for seven to 10 days to see if he comes back on his own.

My mom and I were stunned.

My dad interjected, "Let me go. If I'm not going back to work, let me go. I'm not going to be a burden to my family. Let me go."

I asked if the biopsy is a must. The doctor said it's not, but in order to treat properly, they have to know what they're fighting against.

She said the antibiotics and steroids are helping him improve. But if we are fighting cancer and not a true infection, this treatment is a Band-Aid and his condition will worsen.

The pulmonologist came in shortly after and was more upbeat and optimistic. She said, "Let's not take it that far yet. These are honest and real conversations we need to have, but he is improving, and we'll take it day by day."

Dr. Sherman, my dad's pulmonologist, will be up on Monday to have broader discussions and a plan for what's next.

The hospital doctor made it sound like this is the end. Whether the biopsy takes him out, or we get his oxygen stable enough, and he goes home with oxygen—he'll eventually suffocate as the cancer continues to spread and takes over his respiratory system.

The doctor left the room.

I crawled in the bed with my dad, tucked myself up under him, and silently cried.

Feeling his body, warm and with life moving through it. Knowing, soon, his spirit will leave him.

It will leave us.

Soon.

Sooner rather than later, I guess I should say.

He got in pep talk mode and told me, "We'll see Sherman Monday and go from there. He's leading this thing, and we're following his lead."

I'm going to lose my dad.

Maybe not today. Or tomorrow. But I will lose him in the near future.

He's suffocating.

His body is shutting down on him.

The machines and medicine are serving him well right now.

We're actually getting to talk to him and him talk back. But he can't stay at the hospital forever.

If they can't stabilize him long enough to fight the cancer, he can't fight the cancer.

And even if he's fighting cancer, that doesn't fix the heart failure.

I've been telling him to hold on this whole time.

But today, I looked him square in the eye and said—

"Dad. Hold on. Keep fighting. But if you're tired and you want the risk of the biopsy, in hopes that once they put you to sleep, you won't wake back up—I understand."

All the options suck.

The ones we have right now.

They suck.

We completed the paperwork with, "Do not resuscitate."

Last night, my dad was talking to his nurse, Josh, about his condition.

He told him—

"Man, I've lived a good life. Fifty-four great years. I've got three good kids that I'm proud of. Been married to the same woman for 35 years. I've had a good run. And when I get there and see the Good Lord, I'm going to thank Him for every day He gave me."

It's still not over. It'll be over when it's over. But there are a lot of obstacles right now.

And a very weak and tired man who has to decide where he's at on this journey.

His journey.

It's not looking too good.

My dad reached into the drawer of his bedside table, pulled

out my book, handed it to me and said, "Here. I read your book. I still don't understand it."

He absolutely does not understand anxiety.

He always says, "Why worry about shit you can't do nothing about?"

I don't even care if he understands or not.

He read it.

That's what matters.

When I became an author one of the most bizarre discoveries I made was that those closest to you will not read your work.

I got a message the other day from someone in Europe who read my book.

That's not uncommon, actually.

But people in the circle around me—not so much.

What does the Good Book say? A prophet is of no honor in his own home?

That's okay.

I'll wait till they're tied down and force them to read.

Kidding.

Maybe.

Progress.

Dad's off the hospital grade oxygen and getting moved to a *regular* room.

And he's grumpy about it.

He's complaining because he's not getting waited on like he was downstairs in CCU.

I said, "Dad. You get to be more independent up here."

He goes, "Nah. Those motherfuckers drop you off here and leave you."

I can't deal with him.

Settled in and getting a breathing treatment.

Tomorrow we will hear from the pulmonologist.
But for today, some progress was made.

The sun has left the horizon.
As I stare at the sky tonight.
The light show begins.
Reminding us of what once was.
Today's hangout with Dad was not earth shattering or filled
with philosophical talks.
We watched TV.
Talked on the surface here and there.
Shared his dinner and dessert.
He ordered an extra cheesecake for me.
Then he slept on and off while I checked in on some work.
We filled the silence with our presence.
Words weren't needed today.
Just silence and leaning in.

Staring at a beautiful sunset.
This is why I don't close my eyes as I endure this crazy roller coaster.
This is why I lean in.
I don't want to miss this.
The beauty among the chaos.
You only get these colors once the sun is fading.
May we never lose our wonder.

I know I write these really deep updates that are gut wrenching
at times.
That's because this whole process is gut wrenching at times.
However, it's filled with so much beauty.

So much depth.

So much hope.

Even if the outcome is not what we hope for—the grace and love that surrounds my dad's life leaves me speechless at times.

I have watched people draw near and lean in.

People have shared soothing words.

I also appreciate the fact that if you don't have words, you just don't have words.

I despise inauthentic words.

Words hold power.

You are a powerful tribe of people who have shared very powerful words even in the absence of actual words.

There are so many things I'm grateful for right now. Too many to list.

But, just thinking of how things fall in place is so beautifully mysterious.

You know a powerful Source is working behind the veil.

My dad has the greatest group of friends from his job at Ford Lincoln of Franklin.

My dad worked at Moody's Tire for 30+ years. His friend, Shawn, worked with him at Moody's for a bit.

Shawn left and went to Ford. He called and asked my dad if he was interested in a new job. My dad jumped at the opportunity and came on board.

My dad's employer created a landing strip for him. The whole team has supported him and championed him through this journey.

A couple of weeks ago, Shawn abruptly passed away.

We are all so heartbroken by this news.

And I can't help but think of how Shawn's simple act of getting my dad a job, literally saved my dad and kept him in the game this long.

My dad is absolutely grieved by Shawn's death, but also, I think, comforted in knowing they'll be reunited soon. Whatever that looks like. However, my dad told me the other day, "When I get there and see him, I'm going to knock him upside the head and say, "I'm pissed that you jumped the line, you bastard!"

Being on the front lines of watching a parent slowly die is hard.

It should be hard.

I was texting with my dad this morning and fully know that soon those texts will stop.

Even if I choose to text him still, he won't text back.

I'll be left with a text thread of memories.

Memories.

Something remembered from the past; a recollection.

But that's not today.

Today, he's still here.

In fact, he's doing pretty darn good today.

He got a chest X-Ray this morning. The doctor said it's not great, but it does look better than when he first got there.

Also he's been on hospital grade oxygen, cranked to 40. As of this morning, it was on 12 with plans to bring it lower throughout the day.

So, there is good news being shared.

But ultimately, he's still dealing with some heart failure and metastasized cancer. They think it has spread all throughout his lungs and also his abdomen.

Last night I took a bike ride. Chasing the sunset.

I was trying to get to higher ground to capture some footage and was running out of time.

The sun seems to linger until right as it's setting.

Once it's on the horizon, it goes fast.

By the time I got to high ground, the sun was gone. I was bummed.

But as I stood there and looked out, I realized the light show comes after the sun has left my view.

The colors that moved across the sky were amazing. Even the sky and clouds behind me were majestic.

As I rode my bike home, the sun gone, I was still in awe of the splashes of color that accompanied me.

It was then that I realized, sometimes the sun has to be gone for you to fully grasp the beauty of what once was.

My dad is getting closer to the horizon.

Watching his life set makes me feel like I'm losing my grasp as I try to make it to higher ground.

But I trust that once he's gone beyond the horizon, the beauty of all he is will expand far beyond what we could ever imagine, and he'll add to the painted sky.

Leaving us awestruck and amazed at the glory of God as He calls his son home.

God will not forsake the light show.

My dad will not forsake the light show.

It will be majestic, indeed.

And I'll be there—leaning in.

I'm grateful for the 35 years with my dad.

I'm grateful for you.

I'm grateful for it all.

"Take my ashes and bury me by the Pin Oak tree."
It's where I came from.
Just put me back."

~William Dotson

My dad shared his dying wishes with me today.

He shared them through his own grieving tears.

He's not gone yet. In fact, he's actually making great progress and should be going home by the end of the week.

The Palliative Care PA came to see him today. She's working to get him relief from his cough. She's put him on a low dose of morphine. Her goal is to help him find comfort.

The Physical Therapist came by to help dad get up out of the bed, walk, and sit in the chair.

He hasn't moved from the bed for a week.

Dr. Sherman, his pulmonologist, came to see him this morning. We asked him if the scan is showing cancer in my dad's lungs.

He said, "It's a shadow all throughout the lungs. This is what lymphatic cancer looks like in the lungs once it fully metastasizes. However, that's also what pneumonia looks like. It's also what infection looks like... but with your condition, if it walks like a duck and quacks like a duck—I think it's a duck."

My dad responded, "So, if this chemo doesn't work, that's my last shot?"

Dr. Sherman leaned in and softly looked my dad in the face and tenderly said—

"I'd say so."

The room was quiet as my dad nodded his head in acceptance of what Dr. Sherman just shared with him.

There's just something about hearing what you already know to be true.

The next step—we need this damn chemo to work and hold this disease off so we can have him a little longer.

Or—honestly, we just need this disease to hurry up. Stop fucking with him and take him.

Watching the slow progression is really hard.

Dr. Sherman is still not comfortable with doing a biopsy. He'd like to avoid it if possible. So, he got a sample of the blood my dad has been coughing up. He sent it to the lab to see if they can detect cancer cells in the sputum.

That will give us our medical proof.

But we already know.

So does Dr. Sherman.

The plan is to get my dad home before the start of next week. Then to chemo next Wednesday.

He needs two to three rounds to see if it's working.

If this doesn't work... well... I guess we'll cross that bridge when we get there.

Today, the grief is heavy.

Damn, it just comes out of nowhere.

It sneaks up.

I got home from the hospital a little while ago and just climbed in the bed.

Sometimes your mind and body call a time-out, and you need to adhere.

Today has been tough. But he's still enduring.

He's the bravest person I know.

I'm so proud to call him Dad.

I'm so grateful he raised me. Although my teenage years were rough as shit! Those are stories for another day. But let's just say we had a "silent treatment" standoff for about a year. He's stubborn as hell and strong willed, but damn it, so am I. I'm incredibly grateful for the past 10 months. We always had a bond, but this cancer gave me a relationship with him that I never would have had. It gave him more zeal for life. He even tried iced coffee—that's a story for another day.

I don't know what tomorrow holds. But I do know today has been good despite the heaviness.

And we only have today.

I'm clinging to today.

You saved my life by choosing my mama.

I can't imagine how my story would have unfolded without you.

I love you.

Sleep well.

I'll see you in the morning.

Annnnnd he's up.

He just got through standing against the wall.

He stood up and said—

"That's a whole hell of a lot of weight that just went on those feet."

I got the giggles.

He smirked.

He seriously doesn't know he's funny.
Keep on making progress, Dad.
He told the nurse, "I'm going back to work."
Alright, Dad.
Let's get you there.
This is a start.

He's standing.
And he's grumpy as hell today.
He got snippy with the nurse and then looked at me and said, "I just don't feel like being nice today."
Oh, boy.
It's been a long morning already.
But... he's standing up. That's a positive.

My dad got released from the hospital.
He got to go home—finally.

My mom sent me a picture this morning. My dad sitting on the porch. Staring out into the yard.
This is the first time he's sat on the porch in months.
I'm glad he's getting to soak this all in—the little things that we often don't slow down long enough to enjoy.

Well.
He's back at the hospital.
His oxygen dropped to low 60s last night and wouldn't come back up.

My mom had to call an ambulance to come get him last night. He's back on medical-grade oxygen, cranked to 30.

He's alert and talking. But he's also having a lot of coughing spasms and coughing up blood again.

We're waiting on the oncologist and pulmonologist to hear what they have to say.

He's up for his next round of chemo tomorrow, and we're curious what decision they'll make about infusing chemo at the hospital.

My mom said she could hear him coughing around midnight last night—she was in the living room, and he was in the bedroom. She heard him talking to someone.

So, she asked, "Who are you talking to?" Dad said, "Myself." And she really didn't think anything else of it.

Today I asked him what was he saying to himself?

He goes, "Get your ass up." Then he smirked.

Those just might be words to live by.

How often do you find yourself in a challenging situation and demand of yourself:

Get. Your. Ass. Up.

I love my dad's willingness to fight.

He's also in way better condition this time to put up a fight.

We still haven't seen any of the doctors, but he was told his CT scan shows the cancer in the same place it was in the last CT scan. So, it's holding.

The hardest conversation anyone could ever have with their doctor has just taken place.

The sun is setting, friends.

My dad told me to tell you thank you to everyone who has prayed and cheered him on through this journey.

He asked that you don't stop yet.

He's tired, but he wanted you to know his gratitude for you.

The medical team has given him the option to request sedation medication—*when* he's ready.

When my dad makes this request, he will enter his final slumber.

He spent today saying his goodbyes—*just in case* he doesn't get another day.

So many people love and adore him.

His work team rushed up to the hospital and flooded his room.

I overheard him tell one of his friends, "Don't be sad for me. I've had a good life. God's just taking me a little early."

Later I asked my dad,

"Are you scared?"

He said, "No. Not really."

This is so surreal.

None of us want to watch him suffer.

He doesn't want to suffer.

We're getting close to the end.

But for today—

Right now—the light is fading but not gone yet.

He said to me, "I ain't dead yet, Pearl... but the end is near. It's coming soon."

Breathe in.

Breathe out.

Lean in.

⁓

The dark is eclipsing the light.
The family is gathering.
The oncologist says my dad most likely won't make it through the weekend—if even another day.
The end is very near.
Lean in.

⁓

Chasing down the sunset.
Trying to cling to a moment I can't grasp long enough.
Fleeting.
And yet—my soul. It is well.
He's still here.
But not for long.

⁓

The transition has happened.
He never asked for sedation.
It happened naturally.
Before he started falling asleep, he told me he was seeing hummingbirds every now and then.
He's been very awake and alert all day. Then all of a sudden—
He transitioned.
The sun has completely set.
The night has come.
My dad has left his post in this realm.

⁓

His middle name is Homer.
The r didn't fit on his hospital bracelet.

I don't think that's by mistake.

I just realized his hospital bracelet reads: "Home."

Wow.

What a journey.

You fought until the very end.

So stubborn too.

He never asked for the sedation medication.

He wanted to listen to his audiobook.

It happened so fast.

He was completely coherent and *normal*, and then he laid back to rest his head and listen to his book.

I'm so grateful I got to walk this out with you.

I'm so grateful I had a front row seat.

And you let me document all of it.

This was not an easy road to walk.

But I would not have missed it for the world.

I kept my eyes on you. You led the way.

I felt like a journalist asking you a million questions and extracting your feelings from you all the time.

I hope I gave honor to your story and closed it out well.

I love you, Dad.

I had not slept yet from the night before when my dad passed*

The sun set and the darkness fell.

But you know what?

The sun rises again.

For 11 months I have chased the sunsets in a way I've never chased them before.

I've always been drawn to the atmosphere right before darkness falls.

But I've also been drawn to the sunrise and I'm typing this as light is breaking through.

These past few days will be days I'll never forget.

My dad made peace in every area of his life.

People who loved him dearly gathered near him.

He hugged grown men, and they cried together.

He made sure he got an opportunity to speak to a family member he was at odds with for many years.

He said he didn't want to be petty, and it wasn't fair to leave without telling that person he loved him despite their differences.

My brother, Tony, was able to rally the troops on social media and get advanced copies of two new books coming out this summer by one of my dad's favorite authors.

Every nurse and doctor was talking about this at the hospital.

They thought it was so amazing!

My dad didn't get his wish to finish both books, but he did pass away with the audio of the first book playing next to his ear.

The medical staff said his ending would be peaceful for him but hard for us to watch.

They also shared that since his respiratory system was working so hard and with the disease in his lungs, he was not fully expelling carbon dioxide.

As the day progressed he would start to get sleepy and fall asleep. When that happened they were supposed to sedate him and remove his oxygen from his nose. Then we would watch him fall into his final slumber.

There are so many emotions right now in regards to what I witnessed last night.

He was up talking with family and friends for quite a while. He did get drowsy as he was listening to his book, but this has been normal throughout his hospital experience.

We didn't know the end was staring us in the face until his nurse let us know.

As I sit here reflecting, it reminded me of labor and delivery. You don't know when labor will truly start. You don't know when the baby will finally arrive. But you trust your body, and you trust the process—along with medical intervention if/when needed. The last hour felt like moments and yet an eternity at the same time.

We did see him struggle briefly because the nurse was trying her hardest to get the medication started... but it was happening so fast.

Tonight as we watched him pass, it was not him peacefully sleeping.

He was sleeping, but his body was fighting to breathe.

He would wake up and rub his head. Then he'd go back to sleep.

Then he woke up, looked at everyone standing around him, looked over at me and said, "Now, what the fuck is going on?"

He wasn't mad.

He asked as if he was missing out on something.

At one point he woke up and asked for a drink of water.

We gave it to him. He went back to sleep.

His body still fighting. His diaphragm working overtime. His vitals dropping on the monitor above my head.

Then, he pulled at his oxygen. He was taking it off himself. He pulled it out from under his nose, off of his right ear, and was struggling to get it off the left ear. I helped him remove it completely.

We knew this was him saying he was done—on his own time.

What seemed like chaos quickly turned to peace.

He relaxed.

He accepted.

He breathed in.

He breathed out.

Then he was gone.

The ultimate *lean in*.

My dad died with my mom, my two brothers, and me standing around him. Coaching him through. Cheering him on.

It was like having a baby.

There's the extreme pain of labor.

But the ultimate joy of life.

From watching my dad, the transition was the labor.

But there was still the ultimate joy of life.

I've learned that whether life is coming or going—it's not pretty. There's no way to make it pretty. But the outcome is worth it.

My dad's tumor was discovered on July 30, 2019. He battled cancer for 11 months and died on June 19, 2020. He did not go down easy.

Just like the William I know.

I told the oncologist shortly before my dad died, "We wouldn't have gotten 11 months without you."

His oncologist said, "I couldn't have helped get him 11 months without him."

And then as he began to cry, he said, "I'm so sorry he's going through this. He's a great guy, and we will miss him."

I think I figured out why people adore my dad so much.

He's honest.

Well, he's honest, uses few words, and has a very country accent.

He's very simple.

We all crave honesty and simplicity. My dad embodied it.

His one-liners are the best.

Well, as the sun has almost fully risen, I'm making my way to sleep.

My take-aways from last night:

There's no pretty way to die. Whether you go fast or slow—it sucks either way. It's traumatic to watch.

Just like delivering a baby.

It's scary.

It's confusing.

You feel lost and out of control.

You're waiting for it to end—but trying to hold on at the same time.

There's no time to think or feel much of anything—you're just trying to be present. You're trying to capture every detail.

You want to look away but you don't want to miss anything.

Then it's over.

And peace that passes all understanding fills the atmosphere around you.

Then a rush of relief hits you. And the abundance of gratitude fills your heart.

I learned a lot from my dad in the past 11 months. I got to know him better than I ever did before.

This was the most heartbreaking yet glorious journey, and I'm glad he was the captain.

The sun set, darkness fell, and my dad is finally free.

Just know the sun will always set—but it will always rise again.

Mourning may last through the night, but joy comes in the morning.

The morning has come.

My dad passed two days before Father's Day. On Father's Day, my mom and I were at the funeral home making arrangements.

I knew we'd be here at some point.

I tried not to prepare myself too much, because I didn't want to miss the present moments with you.

But I knew this was in the forecast.

I've briefly pictured this in my mind before.

And now I'm standing here.

It's pouring rain outside.

Rain.

When the clouds can't bear the load anymore, and they have to let loose.

Release.

Heavy release.

Without the outpouring we couldn't survive long.

Same with grief.

That energy has to go somewhere.

It has to be released.

Hard.

Heavy.

Violent.

Aggressive.

Intense.

Angry.

Will it ever stop?

Will it ever calm?

The words that come to mind as I listen to this rain slam down.

The tempo of my emotions moving with the tempo of the rain.

Aching.

Steady.

Consistent.

Torrential.

Dense.

Nothing I can do to stop it.

It's nature doing what nature does.

It's the natural flow, flowing.

The same is required with us and our grief.

It's not about being strong.

It's about being brave.

It's about showing up.

Keeping your eyes engaged.

Keeping your heart open.

Breathing when you want to hold your breath.

Relaxing your shoulders when you want to tense them.

Not running from the discomfort.

After a little while, the rain will stop.
At first it will lighten. Then it will stop.
The smell will be in the air.
The trees will drop remnants.
Puddles will linger.
But that wave of grief will subside.
And you'll catch your breath again.
And the heaviness in your chest will lift.
You'll remember you're in the flow.
You are the flow.
Just as the stream has to move, so do you.
The stream doesn't have to be told to move.
It just does. It finds a way.
It's not an option to be stagnant.
Because stagnant stops the flow.
It breaks the natural cycle.
Streams were not meant to be motionless.
I don't mean busy.
Doing.
Going.
I mean motionless.
You are the stream.
I am the stream.
My dad is the stream.
Is.
Not was.
Is.
Along with anyone else you grieve.
They are here.
They are flowing.
They are the stream.
Not were.
Are.
Dad.
You're not gone.
You've just taken on new form.

I see you in the fireflies.
In the rain.
In the streams.
In the buds of the magnolia tree.
In the sunset.
The sunrise.
I feel the warmth of you when I put my hand to the earth.
When my heart beats.
I feel your heartbeat.
You're in my breath.
The inhale.
The exhale.
You're here.
In the melody of the song.
In the lyrics.
In the breeze.
In the sway of the trees.
In the voice of the birds.
In my laughter.
In my tears.
Flowing.
All of it.
You are there.
You are here.
You never left.
You're just no longer contained.
You're flowing.
Happy Father's Day.

Grief.
I've been writing my dad's eulogy.
At first, I thought—well, I've been writing it all along.
But then—I thought—No.
No I haven't.

I've just been narrating a story.

A month ago, when my dad went to the hospital for the first time, he looked at me and said, "Start writing my eulogy." But I couldn't.

It wasn't time.

I knew the energy would be different once he was gone, and therefore the heartbeat of the writing would be irregular if written too soon.

The breath too shallow.

It wouldn't be right.

The right energy encapsulated within the right timing is powerful.

And I don't mean "energy" in some weird way.

Look. We're energy.

We let off energy.

We take in energy.

Vibration.

Frequency.

Whatever the hell you want to call it.

We all feel it.

We all get chills when *that* moment happens.

We all get tears in our eyes when *something* pierces our heart.

We can't explain it. But we know it.

Collective consciousness.

The Spirit.

Heaven touching earth.

The labels don't matter.

That's the problem.

We can't see the forest for the trees.

We bounce from one label to the next.

Anchoring ourselves to an identity made up of labels.

Living out a script that someone else wrote for us.

And we agreed to—because we never knew we had a choice.

And yet our soul cries out from within.

We stuff it full of shame and guilt.

We quiet it with *rights* and *wrongs*.

We calm it by over—explaining in hopes that no one sees us as *bad*.

Because a misunderstood heart is devastating.
Until it's not.
I'm sitting here watching a stream.
I hoped it would spark some creativity to be near the earth.
But as I sit here, I realize the stream understands my grief more than any person ever could.
Because it's not in its way.
It's just being a stream.
Not apologizing.
Not afraid to get it wrong.
Not focused on getting it right.
Not overthinking.
Not stalled out or uncomfortable by my emotion.
It's just there.
Not asking me to, "Let me know what you need."
Or "I'm here if you need to talk."
It doesn't expect me to reach out.
It reaches in.
Just by being in its natural form.
The stream knows what to do because it's not thinking about what to do.
Don't get me wrong, people offer what they know to offer.
And they mean well.
They do.
But we overcomplicate our humanity.
We overcomplicate love.
We take living for granted.
And we look at death as "the worst that could happen."
We don't sit still with the energy.
The energy that holds the answers hovering around our heartspace.
We miss it.
Overlook it.
Because it's too simple.
And we're caught in the labels.
Your mind is not your own until you free it.
Unlearn.

Throw off.

Take back.

And can sit in peace with the energy.

Grief.

There's no true way to describe it.

You just have to sit with it.

And in some odd way—grief—grief itself, will comfort you.

Grief has not come to harm you.

It has come to heal you.

To bring answers through the energy.

The gifts of life are everywhere.

Even among the gift of death.

Embrace the energy.

And lean in with it.

On my Certificate of Live Birth.

The "Father's Name" line left blank.

William wasn't my birth father.

But he was at the hospital when I was born.

My birth father abandoned my mom when she was three months pregnant with me.

William took on my older brother and an unborn child. Claiming us as his own.

Because he loved my mom.

Because he loved her children.

And because that's that kind of guy he was.

When I was 31, I found out about my birth father.

My mom and William gave me a steady *Mom* and *Dad*. So, even with a blank line under *Father* on this certificate—the father I grew up with never left me blank or empty.

I remember the day I went to my parent's house to tell William, "I know you're not my birth father." He was caught off guard. "And!?" He asked, stunned.

I cried and thanked him for saving me.

From what I heard about my birth father, he was a monster.
The best thing he could ever do was abandon me.
I am who I am because of William.
My dad.
Blood or not.
A blank line under *Father* on a piece of paper—
I have never been empty.
I know who my dad is.
William H. Dotson.
I am proud to have been loved and raised by you.

"Be softer with you.
You are a breathing thing.
A memory to someone.
A home to a life."

~Nayyirah Waheed

My mom called me and asked if I was alone.

I was sitting at the table with my kids. She asked if I could get alone.

I walked to the bedroom.

She shared that my dad had been sick for quite a while, and they had gone to the doctor earlier that day.

She started to cry.

"There is a mass in his colon, and they think it's cancer."

I cried.

After we hung up, I jumped in the car and drove to their house.

When I got there, I snuck through the garage and into the house. The door wasn't locked.

My dad turned around and looked at me when I entered the living room. He was sitting on the couch alone.

We looked deeply at each other.

"I'm going to kick your ass!" I said to him.

Then I ran over to the couch, threw myself on top of him, and bawled as I buried my head into his neck and wrapped my arms around him.

I knew right then that time was fleeting. Time was limited. It became more real than ever.

He rubbed my back and let me cry.

"I ain't dead yet, Pearl," he said.

After a short while I stopped crying and sat next to him.

We watched TV in silence. Just me and him.

Every now and then we would look at each other.

Silent.

Gentle eyes.

He knew. I knew.
We hoped for the best.
Falling.
Yet clinging.
Grasping for more time.
The start of his 11 month journey started on this day one year ago.
We should be celebrating him living today.
Living.
Present.
Current.
But instead, I celebrate what was.
Gone.
Past tense.
Memories.
So many emotions on this day one year ago—and thinking about them, I can feel them all.
I don't want to think about them. Let alone feel them.
And yet here they are.
Flooding.
Pouring.
Filling.
And here I am. On the other side. Without him.
Everything I cried about on this day one year ago has come to pass.
But it's the in-between.
Those 11 months.
The joy was there.
The treasure was there.
Love on the deepest level was there.
He was there.
Damn. I miss you, Dad.

There's an ambulance at my neighbor's house.
They are not rushing.
The people standing around were quiet and calm.

I just knew they were going to bring a dead person out of my neighbor's house.

I just knew it.

It's a feeling in the air.

An energy in the atmosphere.

It took me back to my dad's bedside in those final moments of his life.

And I wept.

Then I sat with the feelings. Sitting on my porch. Because something about being near death made me feel near to my dad again... and I longed for that feeling.

I voluntarily threw myself into that grief.

Just to be close.

To be near.

To connect to something real.

To feel something so raw.

I strangely miss the ache and anxiety of knowing I would lose him soon.

Instead of losing him altogether.

Ending.

Ended.

Gone.

Over.

Done.

Pain.

Dull.

Dense.

Empty.

Numb.

God. To feel something so real. To eavesdrop on their suffering. Just so I can be reminded of my own.

I sat here and cried for them. Hiding behind the shadows. Waiting for the corpse to appear on the gurney.

I know this feeling.

I'm certain.

But what emerged from the house was a gurney, pushed by

paramedics, revealing a man with dark hair, with a face mask, sitting up.
Conscious.
Alive.
Coherent.
Calm.
On his way to get help.
Alive.
Living.
Breathing.
Peaceful.
And I weep.
For them. Because their loved one is still alive.
For me. Because mine is dead.
I wilt.
I wilt.
Happy for them. But agony for me.
Maybe I don't know the feeling of death. Or loss.
Maybe I was wrong about that.
Perhaps my judgment is skewed.
Perhaps I just know humanity. Not life or death.
But all of the above.
A gift.
All of the above.
With tears streaming—I'm grateful I can feel all of the above.

I want to forget you.
I want to pretend that you never existed.
I want to forget you.
I wish I could.
So, then your memory wouldn't show up unexpectedly and knock
the breath right out of me.
I wouldn't miss you if you never existed.
I wouldn't ache so bad if you were never here.
If you were never here.

Then you would have never left.

I want to forget you.

Because I don't want to cry anymore.

And not just cry. It's not a typical cry. It's heavy. Reluctant. Overwhelming. Debilitating.

Grief can be an asshole.

The silence of the late night. Nothingness in my mind.

And then you are there.

But you're not there.

Because you're gone.

I want to forget you.

Because if this weight doesn't lighten that's going to fucking suck.

I welcomed this pain when you were here. As you were walking your path to the end. I welcomed it.

I strangely enjoyed it. As much as you can enjoy something so terrible.

The difference is we walked it together when you were here. You comforted me more than I comforted you.

And now you're gone.

These tears are so burdensome.

I can't breathe.

The exhale of cries is long and hollow.

Wailing and moaning says all I need to say.

All I can say.

I want to forget you.

This silent scream that echoes through this room is the only way to release the pain.

Like a pressure valve.

Releasing so I don't explode.

God, I want to forget you.

You should be here.

I miss you.

I miss those 11 months.

Walking with a man through his mortality was radiant. Multifaceted. But radiant.

I want to forget you.

Then I wouldn't be here writing this about you.

I wouldn't be wanting to forget you.

I can't breathe.

I want to feel nothing.

Yet, I feel everything.

In this moment, I feel it all.

You're not coming back.

I watched you die.

You're dead.

You suffered more than you ever let us know.

You endured so you could stay with us.

I miss you, Dad.

The days are getting lighter. Things feel mostly *normal*. The grief has lifted.

But grief doesn't go away. Apparently. It takes on new form. Shows up in new ways.

Unexpectedly.

And heavy as fuck.

Yesterday, I heard the windchimes, and I smiled.

Those windchimes—a gift given to me by a friend. A hummingbird base with windchimes attached and a note that says, "He now flies with hummingbirds."

When they chime, I think of you. I remember you.

If you were never here, I wouldn't have those windchimes. I wouldn't think of you when I hear them—because I'd never hear them. Because I wouldn't have them.

My tears have stopped.

I can breathe.

My shoulders relaxed.

My breath back to normal.

I love you.

I'd never want to forget you.

I'm so glad I had you.

I'm so glad I have you.

Always.

Within.

Around.
Throughout.
I could never forget you.
Nor would I want to.
Maybe you visit me in the grief.
Maybe that's how you show up sometimes.
Maybe you're comforting me, and I just can't see you.
I'll have to get used to this new way of knowing you.
In the silence.
In my breath. Or lack thereof.
Through my tears.
Echoing through the windchimes.
You are here.
You never left.
You just took on new form.
No longer contained.
No longer restricted.
I could never forget you.
Please don't let me.
The stillness of the night has returned. My calm has been restored.
As if this tearful, raging breakdown never happened.
Grief is not meant to be controlled or understood.
Grief just is.
Is.
A verb that expresses existence or a state of being.
State of being.
Just like you.
Just like me.
Being together.
We are here together.
I would never want to forget you.
And I never will.

Still chasing the sunsets.

Even though you're gone.
Even though there's nothing left to chase.
I still chase you down.
Not even 90 days yet.
I focus on catching my breath.
It feels short without you.
How does this ever get better?
Does the pain ever weaken?
I talked to mom on the phone today, and Eric spoke up in the background—and it sounded like you.
It hurt.
The deep ache.
The missing.
The memories.
This life beyond you makes me question if you were ever really here.
You were.
You were here.
Death is bizarre.
Life moves on with or without you.
I have to stop and remember.
Chase the sunsets.
Because you are there.
I remember you there.
I feel you there.
Where are you, Daddy? Where did you go?
I long for that place.
That peace.
The knowing.
You.
You are there.
And yet you are here and there all at the same time.
You surround me.
You lead me to the sunsets.
A private space between us.
Sharing secrets.

You are whole.
Okay.
Well.
Knowing.
There is a space between—but you fill that space.
You see me cry, and you understand—even though I don't.
Teach me your ways.
Continue to teach me your ways.
I'm here for it all.

Longing.
 There's a longing.
 It's always been there.
 I assume it always will.
 Displacement.
 More.
 Different.
 Aching.
 Searching the world for your home.
 Something beyond brick and mortar.
 But no one understands.
 Silenced into perfection. Or the illusion. Because it makes people
more comfortable.
 And we need them to feel comfortable in order for us to maintain.
 Yet we betray ourselves. Our creativity. Our evolution.
 We drift.
 We cling.
 Imploding.
 Longing to exhale.
 Holding our breath.
 Tensing our bodies.
 Clinging to something safe.
 But is it not the free fall—
 The uncertainty—

The wonder—
    that truly sets us free?
May we tear down the walls that divide us from each other.
May we tear down the walls that keep us from ourselves.
Lonely and alone are two different things.
Beautiful.
Like a gem.
The ether speaks in this space.
Downloads.
Uploads.
Whatever.
Whichever.
Taste and see.
Feel.
Energy rising.
Echoing.
Rippling.
May we be conduits of Source.
A secret—only revealed to those who are seeking.
They know.
You know if you know.
The knowing is in the mystery.
And so is the freedom.
Heart to heart.
In the silence.
Freedom.
In the unknowing—there lies the knowing.
Only few will find it.
Freedom.
Etched.
Stained.
Engraved.
Love.
Love.
Simple.
Unscathed.

As it should be.
As it was meant to be.
As it is—
Love.

Lay your hand upon the heartbeat of the earth.
Can you feel it beating?
Can you feel her?
Life upon the elements.
But winter is coming.
Let her come.
Welcome her as a gift.
Admire her timing without resistance.
Observe her ways.
She doesn't overthink. Or hold back. She doesn't doubt or get lost in the confusion.
She loses what she loves.
Knowing it will return to her.
She forgets what was.
But always remembers.
And she moves towards what is.
She doesn't have to ponder who she is becoming—
because she already knows.
Exactly who she's meant to be.
She's always been who she's meant to be—regardless of the season.
Place your hand upon the foundation of the earth.
Feel her warmth.
Know her.
Trust her.
You are her.
And she is you.
Change with your season.
Hands open.
Heart open.

Lower your shoulders.
Soften your jaw.
Breathe in.
Breathe out.
Lean in.

T he moon sends us on a magical journey of hide and seek.
It's constantly changing.
Sometimes it's so bright that you have to squint to embrace its fullness.
Other times it's dim.
In and out through the clouds.
Covered.
Missing.
Or so we think.
Then there are nights like tonight.
Waxing crescent.
A sliver.
Yet it's still there.
And sometimes the sky is so clear that you can actually see the whole moon, but only a portion is reflecting light. The rest is shadow.
Is the moon ever not whole?
No.
Of course not.
It's always been whole.
Nothing changes except the expression of light.
The light determines what we see.
Dad.
Your physical presence diminished four months ago.
I think about you every single day.
Numerous times.
Mostly in passing.
Because—
Well.

Life goes on.
Until it doesn't.
Funny how that works. Maybe that's grace.
A soft landing.
Something so mysterious yet so natural.
Normal.
Part of the process.
The cycle.
Like the moon.
Phases.
Constant.
A game of hide and seek. Knowing it's always there—even when we can't see it.
But on the nights when we do—
It's radiant.
Radiant.
You.
You are radiant.
Full.
Whole.
Majestic.
And even when I only see a sliver, you are there.
Facing the light.
There's so much I don't understand with my mind—
But I know with my heart.
I know.
No words to make sense out of it.
I feel it.
I see you in the crescent.
Radiating light.
I know you in the emotions.
The tears.
The grief.
The joy.
You are expressed far beyond the mind these days.
Keep teaching me how to reflect the light.

Keep showing me wholeness even among the crescent.
Cheers. I raise my Blue Moon to the crescent moon.
We raise our glass—to you.
Four months down, dad.

"Where your greatest discomfort lies is also the spot where your greatest opportunity lives.

The beliefs that disturb you, the feelings that threaten you, the projects that unnerve you and the unfoldments of your talents that the insecure part of you is resisting are precisely where you need to go.

Lean deeply toward these doorways into your bigness as a creative producer, seeker of personal freedom and possibilitarian.

And then embrace these beliefs, feelings and projects quickly instead of restructuring your life in a way that's designed to dismiss them.

Walking into the very things that scare you is how you reclaim your forgotten power. And how you get back to the innocence and awe you lost after childhood."

~Robin Sharma (The 5AM Club)

I sent myself on a two-day writing and creativity retreat.

Amazing how our minds unfold when we're left with ourselves.

I sit here in silence and what do I hear?

Me.

My inner voice.

Not silenced. Or diluted. Or dimmed. Or far off.

Me speaking to me.

No anxious thoughts or worries. No what-ifs or outrageous expectations that I've placed on myself for the next 48 hours.

Just me embracing me.

Among the birds chirping and the fall leaves rustling outside my balcony door—there is me.

With no tasks or to-dos.
No place to be.
No chores in sight.
No interruptions.
There is me and my gift.
Are these two separate things?
Or is my gift simply—me?
There is time.
Time and space.
Essence.
Quiet and stillness.
I am here with me.
Emerging from the newfound sanctuary, these words come forth:
"We are not seeking to heal ourselves.
We are seeking to return to ourselves."
And the magical unfolding begins.
The creativity flows.
The thoughts go beyond thinking.
Beyond logic.
Beyond the programming of what we think we know—what we fight to defend and don't even know why we believe it to begin with.
There is just me.
Returning to me.

Friends, maybe we've been off this whole time. These ideas that we need to heal. Constantly seeking a new healing technique. New programs. New exercises and diets. Products. Therapies. Those are great. But perhaps just another distraction?

What if you're not looking to heal yourself? What if you're simply looking to return to yourself?

You are your answer.

You. With you.

Daddy.
Come back.

I'm not writing it.
I'm receiving it.

~Lenny Kravitz

I've been exploring this new emotion called grief. Of course I've grieved and had loss before— Loss of relationships. Jobs. Being misunderstood. Losing grasp on what I think I wanted. People from afar. I've grieved for sure. But to experience the void where a human—who was active in your life in real-time—once resided is totally different.

Yes, I have been deeply saddened by the loss of my dad since he passed. But I started grieving the moment he was diagnosed. And to be honest, I grieved him far beyond then.

There was no relationship prior to his diagnosis. We weren't at odds. He was just a man who held a placeholder of "dad" when the holidays came or in passing.

He wasn't a bad father. He just—was a man with his own internal stuff. I had no expectations for him to be something for me. I wasn't seeking a missing part of me through him. No person should ever have to carry that weight from another person.

I've always looked at it like, *you get what you get and you can take it or leave it.*

My dad hardened over and numbed to the world years ago. He worked. He came home. He read books. He did work around his yard. He tinkered with cars. And the TV was always on football or Fox News.

But the moment the idea of cancer was mentioned—he transformed.

He woke up from his slumber, and he lived.

He returned to himself.

I loved who he became.

I loved who he was.

I truly loved him.

Not because he held the title of "dad." But because he was merely a complex, wise, fun, and loving human.

He became adventurous.

He laughed a lot.

He was a great listener.

I'd often catch him staring at the things we take for granted.

A tree.

The sky.

I'd catch him staring at me.

He observed to feel. Because for the first time in a long time he was alive.

He cried.

He softened.

His heart opened, and he shifted the energy around him.

So, as you can see—yes—I have grieved and am grieving and will forever in some way grieve the loss of the missing placeholder called "dad."

But greater than that, I'm not deeply wounded by losing my dad of 35 years.

I'm wounded by losing who he became after his cancer diagnosis. I'm aching for those 11 months.

The joy, the love, the humor, all the great meals we shared, and how many times we "cheersed" and drank Blue Moons.

All the learning about each other.

He was my friend.

A new friend yet one of my closest.

He had nothing to lose, and so he didn't care about judgment or holding back. The timeline was short, and he knew it.

So he lived.

Until he died.

And there is so much depth and honor in that.

I am most creative when I'm experiencing something real.

Through this writing retreat, my best writing emerged when I was in the trenches of raw and painful emotion.

The ones we run from.

The ones we avoid.

To enter into and navigate that darkness takes a lot out of me. But the treasures are in the depths of that dark cave.

I spent a lot of time in the cave exploring.

As much as I love the textures of emotions, one cannot live in the cave—one can only visit.

It's a deep dive. Eventually you have to come back up for air.

And light.

And take your place among the living—or among those who think they are living.

Like a washcloth you're twisting to stop the water from dripping. One good twist and it all pours out.

That's what this trip did for me.

By no means am I glad my dad is gone. But because he is, I can anchor to this:

I am forever changed because of him. Not only for the sacrifices he made for me as a child, or the things he instilled in me as my father, or because he battled cancer—

But because he died.

It wasn't just a close call. It was *the* call.

I evolved.

My writing evolved.

And although he's physically gone, our relationship is still evolving. And always will.

This is life.

It's the human experience.

Trying to avoid the pain doesn't stop the pain.

Pain is energy. It has to move. And it will move.

But life is so much more than pain.

It's joy

Pleasure
Bliss
Humor
Connection
Trust
Forgiveness
And more things than I can list.
It's not all just pain and trauma or our mental health issues.
It's not about compartmentalizing, trying to figure it all out, and healing.
No matter how healed we get—we will always be healing.
It's about remembering.
Remembering who we are.
Who we're becoming is simply just who we are.
It's about restoring.
Restoring what was taken. What we gave away unknowingly.
It's about returning.
Returning to the essence.
To our power.
To our birthright.
Ultimately—
We are not seeking to heal ourselves.
We are seeking to return to ourselves.
The answer that you so desperately seek is—
You.
Return.

We buried your ashes by the Pin Oak tree today—just like you asked.

I know you're not in those ashes, so seeing them being poured out didn't hurt.

Is that not what our life is anyway?

A pouring out?

Nourishing the ground where we stand?

The imagery was symbolic.

Maybe some people say final words when they do stuff like this—but we didn't.

We giggled, talked shit to each other, and prayed we didn't see one of your tattooed teeth among the ashes.

We closed out this chapter before the end of the year.

I really haven't felt much lately. I always check in with myself when I feel nothing.

I'm fine. Just transitioning.

Even grief is fleeting.

The chasm of what was and what is—it's getting wider.

And I'm relieved.

Loosening.

Relaxing.

Relief.

Joy.

Vibrancy.

Returning.

Not as I was. But as I am.

Life emerging.

Growing.

Developing

Transforming.

Moving with the wonder of the journey.

Reminding myself it's about pouring out.

Nourishing the ground where you stand.

Because we will live on in others once we're gone.

Dad, I'll carry you with me for as long as I have breath in my lungs. And everyone I touch—you'll have touched.

Circle of life, I guess.

I'm going with it.

Resistance doesn't do much of anything anyway.

The energy of your remains has returned to the earth.

Grounded.

Home.

You are now *fully* home.

2020 attempted to break me.

I say *attempted* because I've been broken before—years ago. And I don't believe people are broken—long term—but I do believe we can break open.

Sitting at the end of 2020 and reflecting back, I realize how fucking hard it was.

Abruptly pulled away from life as we knew it. Social connection halted. So much uncertainty, and yet we held on.

Then my dad's health declined quickly. A few weeks of him battling to live—and then he let go. Just like that he was gone from this earth.

I heard an Old Wive's Tale that says death breeds new life. Once a family member passes, it's not uncommon for someone in the family to become pregnant shortly after.

It's like the perfect surprise ending to a year of heartache and loss.

New life.

Expansion.

Growing.

Evolving.

Restoring.

When I watched my dad die, I compared it to labor and delivery. I said the two are more similar than I could ever imagine. Both messy, awful, scary, and beautiful in their own way.

June 2020—I watched someone I love leave.

July 2021—I'll watch someone I love enter in.

Life is always writing the most beautiful story for us.

My husband has this saying he uses often, "I'm just here for the ride."

Meaning, the ride is moving regardless of what we want and when we want it. Sure, we have small pockets of *control*, but ultimately we're just on the ride. Regardless of our plans, goals, ambitions—the direction and speed can change without notice.

We can resist the changes, or we can throw our arms up in surrender, trust the process, and enjoy the ride.

I'm sitting here reflecting back on 2020, and even though it was hard, I'm grateful. Because honestly, every year has hard seasons. 2021 will have its tough times as well. And we will endure. Just like we always do.

We made it! The eve of a New Year, friends. We made it through together—maybe not physically side by side, but we adapted and adjusted, and we kept going.

And we are still going.

Here's to who we were in the past.

Here's to who we'll become in the future.

Here's to who we are right now.

And here's to my surprise baby that has come right on time.

The perfect ending to this year.

Life emerging.

On July 22, 2021 we welcomed a healthy baby boy into our lives.

Axtyn William Poynter

I'll leave you with a couple of poems I wrote. One a few days before the baby was born and one that I wrote on his birthday.

"*You are safe here.*"

"*You belong here.*"

Two affirmations I always spoke over myself on repeat whenever I felt out of place on my journey.

It took a few years for my body to believe this.

My head understood, but not my body.

The physical manifestations of anxiety always reminded me that I was out of place.

Didn't belong.

Not accepted.

Outcasted.

Yes, these can be straight up lies.

But this is also what happens when you're constantly betraying yourself and forcing yourself into environments that go against everything you are.

When I finally found myself in places and around people that agreed with my soul, I felt ease. A sense of belonging.

But old feelings would move through my body in an attempt to sabotage me.

"You are safe here."

"You belong here."

I'd continue to speak this over myself until every ounce of me believed it and felt it.

Eventually the physical feelings subsided.

It's rare I have to speak these affirmations nowadays.

It's not about reminding or believing.

I just know.

I know it in my knower.

I think of this baby boy that's about to enter into an environment that is foreign to him.

And for his whole life there will be this sense of wanting something more.

Something beyond himself.

Something beyond this place.

That thing that we all feel calling out to us from time to time in the stillness of ourselves.

An invitation to return.

To where?

We don't know.

But we know.

And yet we can't quite put our finger on it with our psyche and walls within our shallow minds.

Like we're not supposed to know with our heads.

Only with our hearts.

Knowing.

In our knowers.

Wherever that may be within us.
Among us.
Around us.
Collectively.
And yet individually.
Somehow separate but not separate at all.
I sit here tonight thinking of new life and I feel grief.
Not what I would expect to feel and yet it's there.
I'm observing.
Not judging.
Just feeling.
Grief.
It doesn't mean sorrow or sadness to me.
It's not about anguish or pain.
It's the feeling of laying it all out there. Letting all the emotions and feelings move freely as they wish.
There's no control inside of this place.
And to try to control it would kill the beauty.
The magic would be gone.
It's a wave that moves.
Living. Breathing. Speaking.
Sharing secrets ... if you'll sit with it and listen.
It has not come to harm or hurt.
It has come to comfort.
Wrapped with the essence of life and all that life entails.
Overwhelming.
Beauty.
Significance.
Overflowing.
Abundance.
Radiant.
All consuming.
Enduring.
Holding.
Releasing.
Breathe in.

Breathe out.
Soften your jaw.
Lower your shoulders.
Let it move.
With you—not against you.
Don't resist the guide.
We are not at war with ourselves.
We are not at war with others.
We are simply afraid to feel.
Afraid we're not safe.
That we don't belong.
And so we create war among ourselves, within ourselves, and then among others.
Looking for something outside of us to bring relief and comfort.
Looking for validation from someone out there.
When all along it's here.
Right here.
Calling out.
Calling you back.
Return.
I feel this life within me.
We anticipate this person's arrival.
Excited.
Thrilled.
So much love.
All that we want for him.
Expect for him.
And he's requiring nothing.
No expectations.
No agenda.
Nothing.
He just is.
Present.
Alive.
No needs.
No wants.

Existing.
Moment by moment.
No striving.
Just riding the wave.
The natural flow of life.
He doesn't think of being safe.
Or belonging.
He has no idea what to expect on the other side.
Or that there is an "other side."
He just is.
Pure.
Untampered.
Whole.
Until he crosses over.
"You are safe here."
"You belong here."
May you know this when you need to know.
In the very depths of your knower.

A year ago, I watched my dad, William, leave this realm.
Today, I welcomed my third baby into this realm.
A surprise baby.
Baby boy.
Axtyn *William*.
I remember when my dad was dying, and the end was drawing near. The nurse said he was transitioning.
The end had come.
I had to get induced today in order to keep me and the baby safe. The plan was to go without pain meds.
I showed up at the hospital 2 cm dilated.
After a few hours and some intense contractions, I just knew I had made progress.
The nurse checked. I was only 2.5 cm dilated.
She increased the Pitocin, and the contractions got intensely bad.
I endured 45 minutes, and that's all I could take. It was just too much. If I hadn't progressed, I was opting for epidural.
The nurse checked. I was at 7 and headed into transition.
Too late for epidural and knowing I had made so much progress gave me a boost of adrenaline—knowing the end of labor was near and Ax would arrive soon.
Transition.
As I dilated from 7 to 8, I cried in between contractions. Not because of the pain, but because I kept thinking of my dad.
Those restful few seconds in between what felt like death—were so special.
Just enough relief to gather my thoughts and catch my breath.
And all I could imagine was my dad's transition out.

The intensity and unknown of it all.

One hour later, I had my baby boy on my chest.

Meeting face to face for the first time.

7-8 was grief.

8-9 was the most physical pain I've ever felt in my life.

9-10 was groaning, screaming, crying, trying to breathe as my body took over and paved the way.

10.

Fire.

Fire and electricity throughout my whole body.

And then.

Relief.

It was over.

Life being handed to me.

Precious life.

I deeply miss my dad—and I'm convinced there is a piece of him within my sweet Axtyn William.

This chapter of life has come full circle.

I have lost.

And I have gained.

From death comes life.

From dark—

comes light.

Radiant light.

For tonight, the sun has set.

Tomorrow the sun will rise again.

And I'm leaning in—

to all of it.

"*This is my body, that's your body.*
This is my mind, that's your mind.
But there's no such thing as this is my life, and that's your life.
If this is a living cosmos—everybody is free to capture as much as they want.
If you capture a substantial amount of life your very presence will become a significant life.
Otherwise you will become a mediocre life.
This is the important thing.
It's not the knowledge you gather in your head. It's not the muscle that you gather in your body.
It's the life.
How much of a life are you?
This will make you significant in your very presence.
If the world gives us an opportunity, we'll do something impactful.
Otherwise, we're just a significant presence.
A huge oak tree standing outside, it is not trying to create an impact.
It is just impactful.
If you go under its shade you feel it.
Otherwise—also it's impactful.
Most people notice it only when it's gone."

~Sadhguru

This is the end and the hardest part of any author's writing journey. Well, there are three hard parts.

Starting.

Continuing.

Finishing.

The end means you're trying to find those magical words that thread and tie all the words together.

You want to leave the reader with so much awe and satisfaction as they flip that last page and close the bent cover one final time.

I'm hoping that will happen here as I write with no direction at all.

I'm believing that will show up here.

I've spent the past two days at my annual writing retreat—alone—in Nashville, Tennessee. About 30 minutes north from where I live.

My goal with spending two days alone was to finish this book.

Two hours and 45 minutes until check out, and I'm still writing. Stuck on the ending.

I think it's because grief has no ending.

And how do you end something that doesn't end?

My expectation in leaving my home was to get into a clear, clean, open space with a good view so I could connect to my creativity.

I was disappointed by the reality. The rented condo is clear, clean and open. But the view—not ideal.

In my direct view is a children's hospital, and adjacent to it is Vanderbilt Hospital. I'm on the top floor of my condo where for two days I have watched LifeFlight helicopters arrive and depart from both hospitals.

Not the most creative view.

In fact, it actually caused me to have a ton of anxiety for the first day and half. This is my first time away from my kids, Trinity and Sway, since mid-November 2020. It's my first time away from the baby in 11 months.

Staring at a children's hospital with LifeFlight coming in and out is not the most settling view.

Last night as I was staring at the cursor on this blank page, trying to find an ending, I kept hearing the helicopters.

I thought maybe they have something to do with the ending of this book, but I couldn't make the connection.

As much as I was disappointed in the view, I thought—

This is exactly where I'm supposed to be.

If I were supposed to be any other place—I'd be there.

But I'm here.

What's interesting is I'm here—writing this book about life.

With a view of LifeFlight.

LifeFlight is a key part of a trauma system. Part of that trauma system is rehabilitation.

The purpose of rehabilitation is to help you get back to living your daily life.

The purpose of this book is to remind you that life was meant to be lived.

To savor.

To feel.

To endure.

To Flow.

There will always be a contrast.

The contrast is what illuminates such depth and beauty.

In some odd twisted way, cancer was my dad's rehabilitation. It's what woke him up to his life. I had never seen him more alive than when he was told he was dying.

We're all chasing the sunset.

Rising in the East.

Setting in the West.

We're all on this journey.

Everyone is.

Maybe this book will help you finally grieve and release.

Maybe it's the LifeFlight your heart needed.
The life-saving transport.
Maybe it's the rehabilitation—reminding you that you still have
life to live—and you should live it.
Now.
Perhaps it's the encouragement you needed to take a leap.
You know you won't be fully alive until you lean into whatever
it is you've been running from.
My plea to you is to live while you're living.
Or—Live while you're dying
Because we're all dying.
We're all chasing the sunset.
That's probably not the ending you were expecting—
Me neither.
But since art was never meant to be perfected—I'm going to
leave it at that and abandon this writing from here.
There is no ending to something that doesn't end.
Even the sun—
It shifts.
It leaves from your view, but it never really goes away.
Just because *you* can't see it—doesn't mean it's gone.
There is no ending to something that doesn't end.
Grief doesn't end.
It shifts.
Life doesn't end.
It shifts.
The presence of our loved ones doesn't end.
They shift.
I don't believe they are gone.
They're just no longer contained.
So much unknown.
So much mystery.
Freedom is in the unknown—among all that mystery.
Keep your eyes wide open
            and
Lean in.

T o my dad, William H. Dotson

Thank you for choosing my mom, Tony, and me—and bringing Eric along too. Thank you for being safe and stable. A man of few words but of strong action.

I am who I am because of you. I will carry you with me always.

I will forever see you in the sunrise and the sunset. You'll be there.

The most beautiful game of tag that we'll continue to play all the days of my life.

Told you I'd put this in a book and share it with the world.

Nothing is wasted.

Nothing.

Love you always,

~Pearl

T o my mom, Melissa Dotson

The older I get, and the more I get to know you, the more I understand. Thank you for your courage. Thank you for choosing me and giving me life, regardless of the sacrifices you had to make and what it cost you. You endured so much to make sure we had all that we needed and could live a good life. I love you.

T o Andrea Eads

You helped me find my voice and my authentic writing style.

This book has come to fruition because of you.

I could never thank you enough for your constant support.

For my birthday in March of 2019, you gave me a book by Danielle Doby, called I Am Her Tribe. *You said her writing style reminded you of my writing style. It was through the gift of Danielle Doby's book and the words you wrote on the inside cover that helped me realize I was a poet.*

You gave me the book in March, and I started documenting this journey with my dad in July.

I grieved and processed through writing poetry.

The poetry you helped me discover.

I'm grateful for your friendship. Also, Daisey is here. Just no longer contained. This season has come full circle. From death comes life. I see you.

~AP

T o Axtyn

You are a gift. The ultimate light in darkness. Thank you for the incredible plot twist.

T o Tony Poynter

Forever, a day, and three hours. No words can ever express my gratitude for you. I will always choose you.

About the Author

April Poynter is a writer, Certified Life Coach, and Corporate Executive.

April is passionate about helping others to explore their thoughts, behaviors and patterns that rob them of their true potential.

In 2019, she founded Blushing Phoenix, an organization for erythrophobia and chronic blushing awareness and support. She has been able to help thousands of people from all over the world navigate their own journey toward overcoming negative thoughts and self-talk regarding blushing.

April is also passionate about women in the workplace being recognized for their efforts and having a voice in the room. In October 2020, she was featured in *Fortune Magazine* regarding "Living Your Truth in the Workplace."

The article speaks to opportunities for women who have chosen the corporate path and how April is helping to create a work culture that elevates women and promotes authenticity among every employee without reprimand, calling all people in her organization to be just that—who they are, fully.

She lives in Middle Tennessee with her husband and three children.

Also Available From

WordCrafts Press

Geezer Stories:
The Care & Feeding of Old People
by Laura Mansfield

An Introspective Journey:
A Memoir of Living with Alzheimer's
by Paula Sarver

First Brush Your Teeth
Grief and Hope in Real Time
by Lisa Espinoza

Confounding the Wise
A Celebration of Life, Love, Laugher & Adoption
by Dan Kulp

Fortunate Son
The Story of Baby Boy Francis
by Brooks Eason

www.wordcrafts.net

Made in the USA
Coppell, TX
24 January 2023

11635615R20089